E.L. DOCTOROW

GARLAND REFERENCE LIBRARY
OF THE HUMANITIES
(VOL. 811)

E.L. DOCTOROW
An Annotated Bibliography

Michelle M. Tokarczyk

GARLAND PUBLISHING, INC. • NEW YORK & LONDON
1988

Library of Congress Cataloging-in-Publication Data

Tokarczyk, Michelle M., 1953–
    E.L. Doctorow: an annotated bibliography / Michelle M. Tokarczyk.
        p.   cm. —(Garland reference library of the humanities; vol
    811)
        Includes index.
        ISBN 0–8240–7246–4
        1. Doctorow, E.L., 1931– —Bibliography. I. Doctorow, E.L.,
    1931– . II. Title. III. Series.
    Z8234.4.T65   1988
    [PS3554.03]
    016.813'54—dc19   88–16106
                                                                   CIP

Printed on acid-free, 250-year-life paper
Manufactured in the United States of America

To my father, Michael Tokarczyk, who introduced me to the joys
of reading, and my husband, Paul Groncki, who has encouraged me
in my work throughout the years.

CONTENTS

PREFACE

This is a comprehensive bibliography of literature by E.L. Doctorow and secondary sources written about or adapted from his work. It includes films based on Doctorow's work and his produced play and its reviews, as well as books, articles, interviews, book reviews and dissertations. French and German material is included and briefly annotated; material published in other Western languages that has been listed in other major reference sources is included, but not annotated. Most of Doctorow's fiction is not annotated, and the material in Part IV is not. The remainder of the entries are.

Part I covers fiction and articles by Doctorow. Entries in the "Political and Cultural Criticism" category deal with political figures and contemporary issues. Entries listed under "Literary Essays" are book reviews or essays that directly address literary concerns. I was hesitant about making this distinction in the nonfiction writings of an author who has stressed that political and social concerns are an integral part of literature, but I did so for the sake of scholars who must categorize material.

The material in Part II of this bibliography often presented classification problems. I decided to enter many chapters or sections of books under "Books" rather than under "Articles," because there are as yet relatively few books exclusively on Doctorow's work. Often it was difficult to determine whether to place an entry under "Articles" or "Book Reviews"; some review essays have been anthologized as articles and treated as part of the emerging canon of Doctorow criticism. If a review essay was several pages long, dealt with thematic questions, and discussed several of Doctorow's works, I usually entered it under "Articles." However, if I regularly found it classified as a review in a source such as the *Arts and Humanities Citation Index*, I entered it under "Book Reviews" to avoid confusing scholars.

In entering book reviews, I have been as inclusive as possible because Doctorow's work, like that of many contemporary novelists, has been much more widely considered in magazines and newspapers than it has been in academic journals. Also, because Doctorow is well known as an author who has both a popular and an academic audience, it would distort his work to omit popular magazines and newspapers. Thus I deliberately omitted only periodicals which I believed scholars would be very unlikely to consult: children's publications, local newspapers with very small circulations, and sensational tabloids. If book reviews were only a few sentences long, they were omitted. When reviews were a paragraph long, I indicated this in the annotations. Whenever possible I have indicated the pages on which a review appears so that readers may have some indication of its length.

The "Films and Film Reviews" section is organized differently from the rest of the material in Part II: rather than being listed alphabetically by author throughout, the film reviews are listed alphabetically according to the film they critique. Most film scholars focus on one of Doctorow's films: they do not examine film adaptations of different Doctorow novels, as textual scholars examine several works by an author. It thus seemed more advantageous to organize film reviews by the film they critiqued. Since I found no film reviews that addressed more than one movie, it was easy for me to adhere to this organization, which would have been impossible in the "Book Reviews" section.

Part III of the book is a somewhat unusual feature for a literary bibliography: it contains carefully pruned selections of readings on the Rosenberg case. As most readers and critics have recognized, *The Book of Daniel* has, as a historical novel, a unique relationship to the Rosenberg case. At times the novel seems to copy the case verbatim; at other times Doctorow clearly invents personages and events. Many scholars who are interested in this book's use of history may need more background on the Rosenberg case.

Finally, at the end of the document is a list of additional sources which were either unavailable to me or of which I learned too late to include in the text of the bibliography. With these few exceptions, the material included in this bibliography has been examined by me.

The major reference materials I used in preparing this bibliography are:

> *Arts and Humanities Citation Index*
> *Book Review Index*
> *Contemporary Authors*
> *Dictionary of Literary Biography*
> *Dissertation Abstracts International*
> *Film Review Annual*
> *Forthcoming Books in Print*
> *Index to Book Reviews in the Humanities*
> *MLA International Bibliography*
> *Reader's Guide to Periodical Literature*
> *The New York Times Index*
> *The Times Index*

Frequent communication with E.L. Doctorow, his graduate assistant Nathaniel Penn and correspondence with other Doctorow critics was also essential in shaping this bibliography. For those who want an overview of Doctorow's career, I have provided a chronology of important events. Biographical information on Doctorow is still scarce; the best sources for it are *Contemporary Authors*, *Dictionary of Literary Biography*, and many of the interviews Doctorow has given.

As I complete this project, I think of how much I considered myself a Doctorow scholar and critic a year and a half ago and how much I have learned since then. It is my hope that those who use this bibliography will likewise come away from it with a greater appreciation for Doctorow's work and the diverse approaches that can be used to investigate it.

ACKNOWLEDGMENTS

There are a number of people who helped to shape this bibliography. Jack Ludwig suggested the project and, more important, helped to develop my understanding of Doctorow's work during my formative years as a graduate student. My plans for this book could not have been realized without the editorial assistance of Paula Ladenburg and her predecessor Pamela Chergotis, who answered numerous questions and offered constructive solutions to thorny problems.

I was also fortunate to receive extensive assistance from friends and colleagues. Paul Heacock read the draft manuscript with an editor's eye and a friend's patience. Sharon Jessee, a critic and scholar of contemporary literature, critiqued the introduction. Paula Uruburu searched for references in the Hofstra University Library, saving me valuable time.

In my search for German translators, I found people whose scrupulousness and awareness of idiom was exceptional: Dorothea Matthaeus and Annerose Dahl.

Some of the most valuable input into this book came from E.L. Doctorow himself, who regularly kept me informed of scholars' work and of his forthcoming projects. His graduate assistant, Nathaniel Penn, meticulously searched data bases and helped me to update the primary sources section of this bibliography.

I also received considerable assistance from librarians at the Research Center of the New York Public Library and some of the New York Public Library's Manhattan branches, as well as from librarians at the New York University and Rutgers University libraries.

Finally, I thank my spouse, Paul Groncki, for teaching me many computer functions, helping me to develop confidence in my computer skills and, as always, encouraging me in my work.

Michelle M. Tokarczyk

INTRODUCTION

One of the things that makes E.L. Doctorow's work interesting to scholars is that it eludes classification: Often when
it seems possible to make generalizations about his writing,
his work changes. In the close to thirty years he has been
a published writer, Doctorow has written in several genres--
the Western, science fiction, historical novels, short stories,
bildungsroman. After the publication of *Welcome to Hard
Times* (1960), *The Book of Daniel*, *Ragtime* and *Loon Lake*
(1980) critics and reviewers began to treat Doctorow as a
historical/political novelist. Then in 1984 the novella *Lives of
the Poets*, in a collection by that name, marked a shift to
the autobiographical that was continued by *World's Fair*
(1985). *The Book of Daniel* (1971), which brought Doctorow
critical acclaim, was marked by its complexity and often-
academic tone. This novel was followed by *Ragtime* (1975),
which was widely praised by reviewers for its inventive
prose and became a best-seller.

The prose style in Doctorow's mature work has
likewise continually varied and often been experimental.
Critic Arthur Saltzman refers to such experimentation as
Doctorow's "stylistic energy," meaning that while Doctorow
deals with social issues in the naturalistic vein, he has been
as stylistically innovative as any of his postmodern
contemporaries.[1]

Doctorow did not start out as an experimental novelist.
His early novels--*Welcome to Hard Times* (1960) and *Big as
Life* (1966)--were traditional. In writing *The Book of Daniel*,
however, Doctorow struggled to render the complexities of
the atom spies trial and, as he often recalls, read the first
one hundred pages of a draft in utter boredom and tore
them up in despair. Then he went on to write the account
in Daniel's voice, and to invent a style that would capture
this character's torment and depth. To do so, Doctorow
continually had to shift person and point of view, and include many digressions, such as descriptions of different
kinds of capital punishment and meditations on the nature
of sequential events.

It seems that through such innovations he not only
created an extraordinary book, but also realized he could
expand the possibilities of fiction. Each of his later works
is, in its own way, stylistically innovative. *Ragtime*'s prose
seems to mock that of history books:

Across America sex and death were
barely distinguishable. Runaway
women died in the rigors of ecstasy.
Stories were hushed up and
reporters paid off by rich families.
One read between the lines of the
journals and gazettes. (p. 4)

World's Fair, a *künstlerroman*, attempts to render the perceptions of a young child, often as recalled when he is
grown. Memories of other family members are interspersed
with the boy's recollections, giving the novel both a scope
often missing from the *künstlerroman* and a sense of oral
history. For example, Edgar's mother Rose at one point
says: "It was at this time, I think, that your father got interested in gambling, in card playing, and I think it was
Markel's doing. Dave had a zest for adventure, he always
dreamed of a big killing." (pp. 74-75)

Whatever the impulse behind Doctorow's experimentation, his style does not limit his fiction's accessibility. Doctorow is one of the contemporary novelists whose work
reaches both popular and academic readers. A quick glance
through this bibliography will reveal that his books are
reviewed and discussed in popular periodicals such as
Vogue and *Newsweek*, as well as in academic journals such
as *South Atlantic Quarterly* and *Genre*. This mixed reception, one suspects, is to Doctorow's liking, for he has
expressed the hope that he would have a following among
common people: In an interview after *Ragtime*'s publication
he said: "... literature, after all, is for people, not some
secret society."[2] When explaining his willingness to work on
a movie based on this book after being extremely displeased
with a film adaptation of *Welcome to Hard Times*, he noted
that film is a form of entertainment that can reach many
people.

This blurred distinction between popular and
academic reception is in keeping with Doctorow's own blurring of genres. Like a documentary novel, *The Book of
Daniel* draws heavily on the facts of the Rosenberg case;
however, it clearly invents things such as the relationship
between the accused couple and the informer and the
psychological states of the children. The result is a dis-
tinct type of historical novel that seems to fictionalize the
documented past.[3] In *Ragtime* Doctorow strove to write a
novel that would not have what he sees as the narrative
closeness of modern fiction, but rather would approximate
the distance of a historical chronicle.[4] *World's Fair* (1985),
as previously mentioned, incorporates elements of autobiography and oral history. Doctorow's work thus continually
redefines the genre of the contemporary novel.

Introduction

What makes his genre-blurring and stylistic experimentation so exciting is, as Saltzman points out, they never seem like mere stylistic play, as does the work of some other contemporary novelists: Doctorow's innovations are always coupled with a firm thematic purpose. *Welcome to Hard Times* has been described as a parable about the struggle between good and evil acted out on the stark landscape of the American West.[5] *World's Fair* portrays, among other things, a boy's maturing to accept and assert his ethnic identity: After having been beaten by anti-Semitic bullies, the character Edgar writes his prize winning theme on the typical American boy: "If he is Jewish he should say so. If he is anything he should say what it is when he is challenged." (p. 244)

Doctorow's ability to combine characteristics of realistic and experimental fiction possibly was shaped by his unique background. He grew up in the 1930s in New York City, the grandchild of a socialist who continually engaged in political debates and who communicated to his grandchild a longing for social justice. Upon entering Kenyon College as an undergraduate, Doctorow encountered somewhat different priorities. He studied criticism and philosophy with John Crowe Ransom, one of the foremost New Critics; and received an education that emphasized a respect for the craft of fiction, and a disdain for works which were regarded as mere polemical tracts. In his fiction Doctorow has incorporated the best from what he describes as a productive tension between the desire for aesthetic excellence and social relevance.[6]

Doctorow's work is particularly noteworthy for grappling with social and political issues. *The Book of Daniel* is not only about the Rosenberg case, but also about the friction between America's Old and New Left. *Ragtime* deals with the plight of immigrants, racism and women's issues. *Loon Lake* has been termed an inverted Horatio Alger story in which a poor boy gets rich by his ruthlessness and cunning. Such overt political and social criticism has led some reviewers and critics to see his work as polemical.[7] In fact, however, much of Doctorow's fiction refuses to take easy political stands.[8] *The Book of Daniel* condemns the radicals as well as the United States government. The novella *Lives of the Poets* suggests writers are not so much victims of their society as of their own self-absorption.

The depth of Doctorow's work is consistent with his own vision of the novel. While he is obviously interested in political issues and social justice, Doctorow does not write primarily to represent partisan views or causes. Rather, he writes about politics because he wants his art to encompass many facets of life. In an interview he stated: "I think art and life make each other. Henry Miller said 'We should give art back to life.' I believe that. I believe more than that."[9] Often Doctorow speaks in admiration of writers such as Tolstoy whose work had great scope and tackled major questions.

One of the most resonant of these questions is how to bear the burden of the past. Throughout his work, Doctorow communicates that neither individuals nor nations can escape their heritage. In *Welcome to Hard Times* the survivors of a town burnt to the ground try to build anew, but are thwarted by a legacy of hatred and selfishness. *The Book of Daniel* depicts the children of a couple executed for atomic espionage grappling with their deceased parents' case. And *Lives of the Poets* is often described as a novella about a man in the midst of a mid-life crisis--a crisis which implies a need to understand one's past and contemplate one's future.

At their best, Doctorow's works are examinations of broad philosophical and psychological issues. *Big as Life* (1966) and *Drinks Before Dinner* (1979) explore how human beings live with the fear of imminent destruction. *Welcome to Hard Times* and *The Book of Daniel* are meditations on the nature of knowledge and history. The novella *Lives of the Poets* tackles the age-old question: How does one live as a good person?

Often Doctorow's work investigates people's development in crisis. The most powerful narrative in *Ragtime* is that of Coalhouse Walker's radicalization in response to injustice. *Lives of the Poets* depicts a writer's struggle to make sense out of his apparently haphazard life. And *World's Fair* is based upon the premise that a child continually perceives and contemplates things around him, regardless of how painful the events might be.

It seems that Doctorow is particularly interested in the effect of suffering on people. In interviews he has expressed his belief that, contrary to some popular wisdom, suffering certainly does not ennoble human beings,[10] and his work certainly suggests this view. In *Welcome to Hard Times* and *The Book of Daniel* characters are permanently scarred and their personalities warped by their horrible experiences. In *Drinks Before Dinner* the Secretary of State's vision is that in the event of nuclear warfare likely childhood survivors will be selected, but they and their children will have traces of horror upon them, and suffer horrible dreams. One day "...those dreams will come true...because the children of the survivors will build a new earth with the genius of conspiracy of survival." (p. 50)

While Doctorow's work examines philosophical and psychological issues, it also deals with personal ones, such as familial dynamics. All of Doctorow's fiction deals with the richness and turbulence of family life (although the family arrangements are sometimes unconventional). *The Book of Daniel* gains much of its force from its presentation of an orphaned son's desire to learn the truth about his executed parents. The novel *Ragtime*, as many have pointed out, is essentially the story of three families--one upper-middle class and white, one Jewish immigrant, and one black American--and the stresses they each undergo because of social forces. Likewise, in Doctorow's most recent fiction-- the novella *Lives of the Poets*, the book *World's Fair* and short stories such as "The Writer in the Family" and "Willi"--individuals struggle with difficult familial relation- ships.

What ties together the diverse themes in Doctorow's work is its strong narrative. Throughout his career Doc- torow has been convinced of the power of narrative: Like many theoreticians, he sees it as a way of structuring ex- perience. In his often-quoted essay "False Documents," he claims,"...there is no fiction or nonfiction as we commonly understand the distinction: there is only narrative."[11] Be- cause narrative has such power, writers must utilize it to its fullest. In his review of Milan Kundera's *The Unbearable Lightness of Being*, Doctorow expresses skep- ticism about Kundera's repeated intrusions into the narra- tive. While many of Doctorow's own works employ narrative intrusions, they do so to stretch the narrative to its limits, to make it work in different ways as, for example, the com- puter printouts and biography of Joe at the end of *Loon Lake* force readers to reinterpret the story. From *Welcome to Hard Times* to *Lives of the Poets*, Doctorow's work is marked by a strong plot that captures readers' interest. It is undoubtedly the strong narrative line in *Welcome to Hard Times*, *Ragtime* and *The Book of Daniel* that made them at- tractive to filmmakers.

Doctorow's work also lends itself to film because of his vivid pictorial imagination. Some reviewers claimed that the novel *Ragtime* itself read like a movie. Anthony Dawson, for one, found that its prose style and motifs of duplicability and volatility were related to film techniques.[12] Others commented on its sweeping panoramic depiction of life in pre-World War I America: figures and events snapped by much as do Tateh's silhouettes. In this novel and in others by Doctorow images are paramount. In *The Book of Daniel* Artie Sternlicht declares he and his fellow revolutionaries will blow the country apart with images. Doctorow likewise relies on powerful, controlling images-- Disneyland in *The Book of Daniel*, ragtime music, the loons and lake of *Loon Lake*--to govern his works. As a contem- porary novelist, he is acutely aware of the effect film and television have had on readers. In an interview with *The*

Miami Herald he stated that writers could not ignore seventy years of optical technology, and perhaps they should anticipate a time when people don't distinguish between books and movies.[13] Such an awareness seems to inform much of Doctorow's work.

Finally, Doctorow's work as an editor and his offices in PEN and the Authors Guild indicate his enduring interest in the situation of writers that manifests itself throughout his work. He has likely been considering these problems for some time because he decided he wanted to be a writer at about age ten. When he first was discharged from the Army, he tried to make a living as a writer, but had to take a full-time job as a reader for motion picture studios to support himself and his family. For many years he worked on his fiction during spare weekend or evening hours. This situation, typical of most authors, indicates their marginality in a society that does not value creative work, but rather, as *Ragtime* suggests, applauds the technological accomplishment of a Henry Ford or the wealth of a J.P. Morgan. The figure of Tateh in *Ragtime* perhaps represents the compromise of the artist forced to contend with material needs.

While pragmatic demands can exact a toll on artists, Doctorow's work suggests, these demands are perhaps not as taxing as artistic requirements themselves. Often Doctorow's novels depict writers trying to create with verisimilitude. In *Welcome to Hard Times* and *The Book of Daniel*, the narrator-authors attempt to chronicle their lives, and in doing so express the difficulty of effectively rendering events. The novella *Lives of the Poets* tells the story of a writer who feels that his success is destroying him, that each book is taking him further away from himself. Sometimes a writer's world is more benign, and at these times its richness is described. *World's Fair* conveys the acute perceptions and sensitivity of a budding novelist. The enduring quality of this child's work is suggested in the image of the time capsule he composes and buries at the end of the book.

As the preceding pages have indicated, Doctorow's work is rich, multifaceted and stylistically challenging. Its virtues have gained considerable recognition in numerous, usually favorable, reviews. *Welcome to Hard Times* was praised for its innovative use of the Western genre and its strong story line. *The Book of Daniel*, which was nominated for a National Book Award, won Doctorow a reputation as a first-rate novelist. *Ragtime* acquired a popular following, partially because its prose style and family themes were so widely praised by popular reviewers. Over the years academic critics have examined its unique fictionalization of history, its experimental prose and its suggestions of the transitory nature of things. Historical fiction written

through *Loon Lake* was generally commended for its blend-
ing of historical facts with imaginative details, and for its
commentary on the American character. Doctorow's more
recent autobiographical work has likewise been well
received: *World's Fair* was given the 1986 American Book
Award for Fiction.
    Academic criticism has evolved more slowly than has
popular criticism. To date, there has been only one book
exclusively about Doctorow's work, one collection of essays
and relatively few articles in academic journals. Existing
criticism has recognized and tackled the scope of Doctorow's
writing. Paul Levine in the "Preface and Acknowledgements"
to *E.L. Doctorow* states that Doctorow writes in the American
romance tradition that accommodates the mythical and the
philosophical. (p. 9) David Gross argues that in Doctorow's
historical novels:

> ...both the power of money and our
> reluctance to acknowledge it are
> centrally significant...the complex mix-
> tures of distancing ironies and direct
> exposure he [Doctorow] creates allow
> him to reveal the hidden sources of
> malaise in our culture more clearly
> than most modern writers.[14]

As the number of Doctorow's works increases (he has a
novel and a collection of essays in press), more critics are
likely to address his fiction. The following pages thus suggest just the beginning of work that will be done on this
author.

1. Arthur Saltzman, "The Stylistic Energy of E.L. Doctorow," Richard Trenner, ed. *E.L. Doctorow: Essays and Conversations* (Princeton: Ontario Review Press, 1985), 75. Paul Levine in the "Preface and Acknowledgements" section of *E.L. Doctorow* questions the rationale for the critical consensus that socially relevant and stylistically experimental novels are mutually exclusive.

2. John F. Baker, *PW Interviews: E.L. Doctorow, Publishers Weekly* 207 (30 June 1975): 6.

3. For a discussion of Doctorow's brand of historical fiction see Joseph W. Turner, "The Kinds of Historical Fiction: An Essay in Definition and Methodology," *Genre* 12 (Fall 1979): 333–355.

4. Larry McCaffery, "A Spirit of Transgression," in Richard Trenner, ed. *E.L. Doctorow: Essays and Conversations*, 39.

5. For examples of *Welcome to Hard Times* as a moral fable see Marilyn Arnold's "Doctorow's Hard Times: A Sermon on the Failure of Faith," as well as Brendan Gill's film review.

6. In conversation.

7. Perhaps the most widely-known review criticizing *Ragtime* on ideological grounds is Hilton Kramer's "Political Romance," *Commentary* 60 (October 1975), 76–80.

8. In his nonfiction Doctorow has often dealt directly with political and social issues. See, for example, "Dream Candidate: The Rise of Ronald Reagan" and "Art Funding for the Artist's Sake."

9. McCaffery, 38.

10. McCaffery, 46, and in conversation.

11. Reprinted in Trenner, 16–27.

12. Anthony B. Dawson, "*Ragtime* and the Movies: The Aura of the Duplicable," *Mosaic: A Journal for the Interdisciplinary Study of Literature* 16 (Winter-Spring 1983): 205–214.

13. Jonathan Yardley, "Mr. Ragtime," *The Miami Herald,* 21 December 1975, 3K.

14. David Gross, "Tales of Obscene Power: Money and Cul-

ture, Modernism and History in the Fiction of E.L. Doctorow," Trenner, 128.

CHRONOLOGY OF MAJOR EVENTS

1931 6 January. Edgar Lawrence Doctorow is born to David Richard and Rose (Levine) Doctorow. Second of two sons.

1948 Graduates from the Bronx High School of Science. Enters Kenyon College to study with John Crowe Ransom. Majors in philosophy. Also concentrates on criticism and acting.

1952 Graduates from Kenyon College.

1952-1953 Does graduate work in drama and acting at Columbia University.

1953-1955 Serves in the United States Army, stationed in West Germany.

1954 20 August. Marries Helen Seltzer. The couple have three children.

1956 Free-lance reader for television studios.

1957-1959 Full-time reader for motion picture studios.

1959-1964 Editor for New American Library. Achieved rank of Senior Editor.

1960 *Welcome to Hard Times* is published by Simon & Schuster.

1966 *Big as Life* is published by Simon & Schuster.

1964-1968 Editor-in-Chief at Dial Press.

1968 Short story "The Songs of Billy Bathgate" is published in *New American Review* 2.

1968-1969 Vice President at Dial Press.

1969 Decides to quit publishing job and devote more time to writing.

Chronology

1969-1970 Writer-in-Residence at the University of California at Irvine.

1971 *The Book of Daniel* is published by Random House.

1972 *The Book of Daniel* is nominated for the National Book Award.

1971-1978 Visiting faculty member at Sarah Lawrence College.

1973 Guggenheim Fellow.

1973-1974 Creative Artists Program Service Fellow, New York State

1974-1975 Creative Writing Fellow at Yale School of Drama.

1975 Visiting Professor at the University of Utah.

1976 *Ragtime* is published by Random House.

Receives American Academy of Arts and Letters Award in Literature.

Receives National Book Critics Circle Award for *Ragtime*.

LHD degree awarded by Kenyon College.

1978 *Drinks Before Dinner* is performed in New York City's Public/Newman Theater.

1979 *Drinks Before Dinner* is published by Random House.

Loon Lake is published by Random House.

Honorary degrees are awarded by Hobart & William Smith Colleges.

1980 *Loon Lake* gets the National Book Critics Circle Award.

1981 Speaks before a subcommittee of the United States House Appropriations Committee on behalf on National Endowment for the Arts Programs.

1980-1981 Visiting Senior Fellow on the Council of the Humanities, Princeton University.

Chronology

1980–Present Visiting faculty, Graduate Creative Writing Program at New York University.

1984 Lives of the Poets: A Novella and Six Short Stories *is published by Random House.*

1985 *World's Fair* is published by Random House.

1986 *World's Fair* receives the American Book Award for Fiction.

1988 Novel *Billy Bathgate* in press.

Collection of articles and reviews in press.

I
PRIMARY SOURCES

A
BOOKS

Novels and Collected Short Works

1 *Welcome to Hard Times.* New York: Simon & Schuster, 1960.

2 *Big as Life.* New York: Simon & Schuster, 1966.

3 *The Book of Daniel.* New York: Random House, 1971.

4 *Ragtime.* New York: Random House, 1975.

5 *Loon Lake.* New York: Random House, 1980.

6 *Lives of the Poets: A Novella and Six Short Stories.* New York: Random House, 1984.
   Includes the title-piece novella, 81-145; and the short stories "The Writer in the Family," 3-17; "The Water Works," 21-24; "Willi," 27-35; "The Hunter," 39-49; "The Foreign Legation," 53-63; and "The Leather Man," 67-77.

7 *World's Fair.* New York: Random House, 1985.

8 *Billy Bathgate.* New York: Random House, forthcoming in 1988.

9 Collection of essays and articles in press.

Drama

10 *Drinks Before Dinner.* New York: Random House, 1979.

Miscellaneous Texts

11 *American Anthem.* Photographs by J.C. Suares; text
   by E.L. Doctorow. New York: Stewart, Tabori & Chang,
   1982.
   A pictorial album of different regions and people which
   celebrates American life.

12 Screenplay for *Daniel.* 1983. See item 478.

13   "The Songs of Billy Bathgate." *New American Review* 2.
      New York: New American Library, 1968, 54-69.

14   "Ragtime." *American Review 20* (April 1974): 1-20.
      Bears some resemblance to beginning of novel.   See
      item 4.

15   "The Pyramid Club." *American Review* 21 (October 1974):
      256-270.
      Resembles section from *Ragtime* on meeting of J.P.
      Morgan and Henry Ford. See item 4.

16   "The Magic of *Ragtime*."   *Sports Illustrated* 43 (14 July
      1975), 56-69.
        Excerpt of novel. See item 4.

17   "Loon Lake." *Kenyon Review* 6 (Winter 1979): 5-13.
      Poem from novel. See item 5.

18   "*Loon Lake*: An Excerpt." *Nation* 231 (13 September 1980),
      219-231.
      Section on Joe's arrest after Red James's murder. See
      item 5.

19   "Loon Lake" *Playboy* 27 (October 1980), 86-88+
      Excerpt on Joe's travels with the carnival. See item 5.

20   "Willi." *Atlantic Monthly* 253 (May 1984), 89-92. See
      item 6.

21   "The Leather Man." *Paris Review* 26 (Summer 1984), 12-
      21. See item 6.

      Carver, Raymond and Tom Jenks, ed. *American Short
      Story Masterpieces*.   New York: Delacorte Press, 1987,
      127- 133.

Manguel, Alberto, ed. *Dark Arrows: Great Stories of Revenge.* New York: Clarkson & Potter, 1985, 103–113.

22   "The Writer in the Family." *Esquire* 102 (August 1984), 8–74. See item 6.

Godwin, Gail, with Shannon Ravenel, ed. *The Best American Short Stories, 1985.* Boston: Houghton Mifflin Co., 1985, 58–67.

Perkins, George and Barbara Perkins, ed. *Contemporary American Literature.* New York: Random House, 1987, 517–525.

Weber, Bruce, ed. *Look Who's Talking: An Anthology of Voices in the Modern American Short Story.* New York: Washington Square Press, 1986, 20–32.

23   "The Hunter." Halpern, Daniel, ed. *The Art of the Tale: An International Anthology of Short Stories, 1945–1985.* New York: Elizabeth Sifton Books/Viking, 1986, 256–262. See item 6.

24   "Hell Gate" *Esquire* 109 (August 1988), in press. Chapter one of *Billy Bathgate.* See item 8.

POLITICAL AND CULTURAL CRITICISM

25 "The Bomb Lives!" *Playboy* 21 (March 1974), 114+.
Posits that the period of America's acute consciousness of the threat of nuclear war ended in the early 1960s. Article attempts to clarify the contemporary understanding of the nuclear threat. Doctorow focuses on his visits to bombers and missiles, describing them in detail, and probing their technological and symbolic qualities.

26 "Writers and Politicians." *The New York Times* 11 April 1976, Section 4, 17.
Taken from an address delivered at the Author's Guild. Compares and contrasts politicians and writers, noting that both are acutely aware of the power of language, but that there is a public distrust of rhetoric, so eloquent politicians often lose elections. Further maintains that politicians have power over their constituencies, but writers do not because in the United States people do not believe literature has power. They think of it as play.

27 "After the Nightmare." *Sports Illustrated* 44 (28 June 1976), 72–82.
Tells of the Israeli athletes being murdered at the 1972 Olympics at Munich and focuses on the response of one victim's wife.

28 "Words into Rhinestones." *The New York Times* 19 March 1980, 27.
Excerpted from testimony given on behalf of PEN before the Senate Antitrust and Monopoly Committee. Speaks against publishing houses increasingly becoming conglomerates, claiming that the concentration of power into fewer and fewer hands inevitably constricts free speech. Moreover, conglomerate values place excessive pressure on publishing houses to make

money, thus jeopardizing the publication of quality literature. Ends by stressing the importance of diverse, uncensored books to any culture.

29   "Dream Candidate: The Rise of Ronald Reagan." *Nation* 231 (19-26 July 1980), 65, 82-84.
      Summarizes Reagan's biography, stressing Reagan's Hollywood experience and consciousness of image-making.

30   "Art Funding for the Artist's Sake." *Nation* 233 (4 July 1981), 12-13.
      Pleads for the maintenance of NEA programs that are likely to be cut by the federal government. Speaks against the "sovietizing" of American life in which people's needs are subordinated to arms build-up. Taken from a speech before a subcommittee of the House Appropriations Committee, Fall 1981.
      Also in item 58, 13-15. Excerpt in item 60.

31   "On the Brink of 1984." *Playboy* 30 (February 1983), 79-80, 156-162.
      Discusses the enduring popularity of George Orwell's *1984*, and claims its appeal is attributable to the book's acute perception of twentieth century statism. Says much of the novel's power stems from its realization that language has the power to manipulate history and present reality. Doctorow then draws parallels between the tyranny in Oceania and the practices of diverse contemporary governments. Posits that there are two poles in the contemporary world--a superstatist one and a humane, feeling one. Only the former could begin a nuclear war, and its heir would be a society mirroring Oceania.

32   "The Bomb Culture: It's a Cold World Out There, Class of 1983." *Nation* 237 (2 July 1983), 6-7.
      Contends that the contemporary world lives in a "Bomb Culture" that is shaped by the threat of nuclear annihilation, and posits the implications of this mindset. Fears novelists have lost power because they can no longer assume an individual's life can transcend the collective fate. Believes neoconserva- tive literary critics are fleeing from the ramifications of the Bomb Culture by extolling novels that deal with private life rather than political questions, and by accusing novelists critical of the United States of being unpatriotic. Taken from an address given to

the graduating class at Sarah Lawrence College, 23
May 1983.

33   "Schultz and PEN."   *Nation* 242 (18 January 1986), 37.
        Protests Secretary of State George Schultz's
having been invited to give an address at the opening
ceremonies of the Forty-Eighth International PEN Conference in New York City.   Argues that Schultz is not
a writer, that PEN's charter specifies the organization
is apolitical and that Schultz represents an ad-
ministration that excludes fine writers from visiting
America for ideological reasons and supports govern-
ments that violate writers', as well as other citizens',
human rights.
Also "On the Literary Congress and Writers: Why In-
vite Schultz?"   *The New York Times*   11 January 1986,
23.
Commentary in item 147.

34   "The State of the Mind of the Union."   *Nation*   242 (22
March 1986), 327-328.
        Examines young writers' obsession with achiev-
ing instant success as part of a national malaise.
Sees America's population on the whole as complacent,
and writers and other artists similarly content to deal
with apolitical, trivial concerns.   Traces these maladies
to the continuing threat of nuclear war.

35   "America's Sacred Text: A Citizen Reads the Constitution."   *Nation* 244 (21 February 1987), 208-217.
        Examines the Constitution as a literary text,
seeing it as sacred in literary terms and probing its
hermeneutics.   Also recognizes the self-interest of the
Founding Fathers and the weaknesses in the original
document.   Relates his ideas to the interpretation of
law and the use of language under Reagan's
presidency.
Also in *Current*   294 (July/August 1987), 8-15.

36   "Tap Dancing Among the Literati."   *The Sunday New
York Times*   Section 2, 4 October 1987, 6.
        Tribute to the late Bob Fosse in which Doctorow
suggests that Fosse had an affinity for writers because they, like dancers, dedicate their lives to performance.

37   "Pumping Out Success."   *The Sunday New York Times*
Section 3, 25 October 1987, 23.
        Written after the record plunge of the stock

market.   Article implies that the stock market's language connotes empty aggrandizement.   The market itself personifies the dangerous American fantasy of
achieving quick wealth without worrying about the
means for doing so.

LITERARY ESSAYS

38   Introduction to Barahemi, Reza. *The Crowned Cannibals: Writings on Repression in Iran.* New York: Vintage Books (Random House), 1977, ix-xv.

        Discusses how the work of contemporary poets who have been tortured runs counter to prevailing American aesthetics which are suspicious of political literature. Examines the prevalence of torture and the world's lack of response to it. Also articulates his conviction that writers have a duty to bear witness to events.

        See also "The New Poetry: The Forms Are Very Strict." *Harper's Magazine* 254 (May 1977), 92-95.

39   "False Documents." *American Review* 26 (November 1977), 215-232.

        The crucial essay defining Doctorow's position on truth in fiction, and the relationship between fictive and nonfictive writing. This piece places the novelist's work in a broadly defined political context. The novelist's use of facts is discussed; important similarities and differences between fictive and nonfictive writing are probed.
Also in item 58, 13-15.

40   Domeny, Katalin. "False Documents," trans. (Hungarian) *Nagyvilag* (July 1988), in press.

41   "Living in the House of Fiction." *Nation* 226 (22 April 1978), 459-462.

        Discusses the author's frustrations with the generic limits of the novel and the writer's need to be socially committed, yet shun polemicism.

42   "The Language of Theater." *Nation* 228 (2 June 1979), 637-638.

        States that *Drinks Before Dinner* was motivated by a desire for a theater centering on ideas rather

than plot. Says the play's language was inspired by Gertrude Stein and Mao Zedong. Article is taken from the introduction to the play.
See item 10, xi-xx.

43   "The Books That Made Writers." *The New York Times* 25 November 1979, 7.
    Responding to the question of what book most influenced him, Doctorow says that his prolific, indiscriminate reading as a child was more important than any single text. Says he began to think of himself as a writer at age ten.
See also *Writer* 93 (October 1980), 25-26. (abridged)

44   "Mother Jones Had Some Advice." *The New York Times Book Review* (26 October 1980), 1, 40-42.
    Review of Mary Settle's *The Scapegoat*. Praises the writer as one of a few contemporaries who has a feel for the forces of the historic moment, and a sense of the individual as both a member of a family and a political being.

45   Introduction to Dreiser, Theodore. *Sister Carrie*. New York: Bantam Books, 1982: v-xi.
    Gives an outline of Dreiser's biography, then suggests that the genius of Dreiser's work is in its depiction of financial status as a key to personal identity. In *Sister Carrie* in particular the novel's strength comes from its portrayal of Carrie as a representative of all human desire.

46   Foreword to *Heinrich von Kleist: Plays*. Edited by Walter Hinderer. New York: Continuum Press, 1982, vii-x.
    Posits that Kleist's plays have an enduring appeal because they center on the nature of consciousness. Narrative energy is another important quality of his work; the quickness of change and power of authorities are important themes.

47   "The Novelist Who Was Born Old." *The New York Times Book Review*, 4 December 1983, 9+.
    Review of *An Amateur Laborer*, an unfinished biographical work by Theodore Dreiser. Suggests that Dreiser's early work is interesting because this author's sophistication and intellectual understanding actually declined as he grew older. Draws parallels between some of Dreiser's experiences and Hurstwood's in *Sister Carrie*.

48 "Four Characters Under Two Tyrannies." *The New York Times Book Review*, 29 April 1984, 1, 45–46.
   Review of *The Unbearable Lightness of Being* by Milan Kundera. Discusses the novel as one written in the postmodernist genre that distrusts narrative and draws attention to the act of composition. Extols its prose, but finds the intrusions into the narrative limiting and believes some broad images don't hold up under examination. Concludes by applauding Kundera's ability to avoid the trap of being merely an exiled writer, a trap substantially different from the American writer's temptation to avoid political content.

49 "The Passion of Our Calling." *The New York Times Book Review*, 25 August 1985, 1, 21–23.
   Laments the lack of social commitment and the narrow scope of much contemporary American writing. Argues that novelists are writing as they live--in submission to society. They should write work that may be less polished, but takes on larger themes.

   See also "The Beliefs of Writers." *Michigan Quarterly Review* 24 (Fall 1985): 609–619.

50 "Braver Than We Thought." *The New York Times Book Review*, 18 May 1986, 1, 44–45.
   Review of Ernest Hemingway's *The Garden of Eden*. Gives an overview of Hemingway's style and strength as a writer. Praises this book's characterization of Catherine Bourne and its tense dialogue. Believes, however, that this previously unpublished novel falls short of its promise. In particular the prose is "bad Hemingway": painfully sparse. Conclusions about the work are difficult to form, however, because we cannot know how Hemingway would have developed and edited this work.

51 "The Importance of Fiction, Ultimate Discourse." *Esquire* 106 (August 1986), 41.
   States that fiction is rooted in a sense of narrative and the novelist has a unique ability to capture the truth about people and situations.

II
SECONDARY SOURCES

E

BOOKS

52 Friedl, Herwig, and Dieter Schulz, ed. *E.L.Doctorow:*
    A Democracy of Perception: A Symposium with and on
    E.L. Doctorow. Essen: Blaue Eule, in press.
    Contains items 66, 69, 73, 84, 94, 95, 97, 113, 120, 141,
    143, 156.

53 Gardner, John. *On Moral Fiction.* New York: Basic
    Books, 1978, 78-79.
    Argues that true morality, which requires sym-
    pathy and responsible judgment, is lacking in most
    contemporary fiction. In brief discussion of *Ragtime*
    Gardner asserts that although the novel seems to urge
    social justice, the characters' unrealistic lives prompt
    readers to be suspicious of all the book's content, in-
    cluding its social statements.
    Adapted in "Moral Fiction." *Saturday Review* 5
    (1 April 1978), 29-33.

54 Girgus, Sam B. "A True Radical History: E.L. Doc-
    torow." Chapter 9 in *The New Covenant: Jewish*
    Writers and the American Ideal. Chapel Hill and
    London: University of North Carolina Press, 1984,
    160-182.
    Argues that Jewish history in the United States
    was transformed by the notion of American ideals, and
    Jewish intellectuals in turn helped to modernize and
    sustain the American idea. A Nietzschean view of his-
    tory is applied. The author sees a "New Covenant"
    response in writers who fault America for not living
    up to its ideals. This tradition culminates in the work
    of Doctorow and Mailer. The chapter on Doctorow
    mentions *Ragtime* and briefly discusses *Welcome to*
    Hard Times and *Loon Lake.* It focuses on *The Book of*
    Daniel as a great Jewish-American novel and explores
    its Biblical parallels, particularly in the context of
    being about Jews in a foreign land. This chapter
    suggests that the character Daniel finds the meaning

of his parents' death in a Jewish context. Girgus further thinks that the beliefs of Paul Isaacson and Robert Lewin represent different meanings of America to Jews.

55 Levine, Paul. *E.L. Doctorow.* New York and London: Methuen & Co., Contemporary Authors Series, 1985.

The evolution of key themes in Doctorow's work from *Welcome to Hard Times* through *Loon Lake* is examined. Topics discussed include the relationships between history and the imagination, elite and popular culture, and political context and experimental style. The book also includes an appendix on film adaptations of Doctorow's novels. The first book-length critical work on Doctorow.

56 *Proceedings of the Belgian Luxembourg American Studies Association Conference.* Ghent, 1987. Contains item 155.

57 Strout, Cushing. *The Veracious Imagination: Essays on American History, Literature and Biography.* Middletown, Connecticut: Wesleyan University Press, 1981.

"Radical Religion and the American Political Novel," (Chapter 5, 70-91). See item 148.

"Hazards of the Border Country: Some Contemporary Historical Novels," (Chapter 9, 157-182).

States that *The Book of Daniel* renders an important passage in the history of the Jewish American Left. In a discussion of the similarities between the novel and the Rosenberg Case, Strout contends that the novel challenges the views of Leslie Fiedler and Robert Warshaw. (See items 536 and 551.) He further contends the novel puts the case in long-range historical perspective; thus the novel ultimately depends upon historical existence of the Rosenberg Case.

"The Antihistorical Novel," (Chapter 10, 183-196).

Sees *Ragtime* as a novel that spoofs the conventional historical novel and casts doubt upon intelligibility of history. Discusses anachronisms, such as Coalhouse's terrorism. Finds the unexamined mingling of fact and fiction without a clear purpose to be an abuse of the writer's imaginative license and detrimental to the novel.

58 Trenner, Richard, ed. *E.L. Doctorow: Essays and Conversations.* Princeton, New Jersey: Ontario Review Press, 1983.
 A collection of interviews with E.L. Doctorow, essays by him, and articles about his work. Covers novels from *Welcome to Hard Times* to *Loon Lake.* As the first collection of criticism, it establishes major approaches to the historical novels. Contains items 30, 39, 64, 78, 79, 85, 87, 91, 101, 119, 140, 171, 173, 183.

59 Ugrinsky, Alexej, Frederick J. Churchill, Frank S. Lambasa and Robert F. von Berg, eds. *Heinrich von Kleist Studies* (Hofstra University Cultural and Intercultural Studies), New York: AMS Press, 1980. Contains items 89, 107.

60 *A Writer in His Time: A Week With E.L. Doctorow.* Davenport, Iowa: Visiting Artists, Inc., 1985.
 A collection of four critical papers that were presented during a symposium on "The Writer and Society" at which Doctorow was a featured writer. Contains items 74, 103, 106, 124. An excerpt from item 30 is also included.

F
ARTICLES

⊦ 61 Aaron, Daniel. "Fictionalizing the Past." *Partisan Review* 47 (2) (1980): 231-241.
      Discusses *Ragtime* and several other books in a review essay on contemporary historical novels. Criticizes a contemporary tendency to fictionalize history because this trivializes it. Sees *Ragtime* as a surface pastiche of genres and a blend of popular and highbrow writing. Concludes that many historical novelists, like political figures, create fantasies that greatly simplify events. While such novelists' work may not have literary resonance, it might be interesting for cultural reasons.

   62 Alter, Robert. "The American Political Novel." *The New York Times Book Review* 10 August 1980, 3.
      Discusses different kinds of political novels. Sees *The Book of Daniel* as a typical "adversarial" political novel which portrays the American system as thoroughly corrupt. Believes that the novel's artistic integrity is ultimately destroyed by its polemicism.

   63 Anastasiev, Mykola. "Jekst romany Y Kontekst literatury." *Vsevit: Literaturno-Mystetskyi ta Hromads ko-Politychnyi Zhurnal* 2 (February 1982): 144-147.

   64 Arnold, Marilyn. "History as Fate in E.L. Doctorow's Tale of a Western Town." *The South Dakota Review* 18 (Spring 1980): 53-63.
      Speculates that the settling, destruction, rebuilding and final destruction of the town is a metaphor for the historical cycle. The novel's main concern is the force of the past and the role of the historian in recording it. *Welcome to Hard Times* looks at historical processes through the vision of the main character who records events, and the book ultimately suggests that such processes tend to create

65 ------. "Doctorow's *Hard Times*: A Sermon on the Failure of Faith." *Literature and Belief* 3 (1983): 87-95.

Argues that the town of Hard Times is a microcosm for all civilizations, and Blue's record symbolically analyzes the causes of all civilizations' rise and fall. Through religious allusions and imagery, *Welcome to Hard Times* suggests civilizations fall when religious beliefs and principles are inverted.

66 Bach, Gerhard. "Novel as History and Film as Fiction: New Perspectives on Doctorow's *Ragtime*." See item 52.

67 Bakker, J. "The Western: Can It Be Great?" *Dutch Quarterly Review of Anglo-American Letters* 14 (2) (1984): 140-163.

Briefly discusses *Welcome to Hard Times* as a Western that treats traditional Western themes, such as the birth of a settlement and the notion that the Westerner is a bearer of civilization, with a post World War II perspective. This novel suggests its settlers' vision was flawed from the start because their motives were wrong.

68 ------. "E.L. Doctorow's *Welcome to Hard Times*: A Reconsideration." *Neophilologus: An International Journal of Modern and Mediaeval Language and Literature* 69 (July 1985): 464-473.

Argues that this novel is underrated. Says *Welcome to Hard Times*, like Doctorow's other novels, is informed by perceptions of history which are unique to the contemporary era. By comparing *Welcome to Hard Times* to James Fenimore Cooper's *The Pioneers*, Bakker suggests that Doctorow's novel depicts the West as a pernicious place rather than a land of possibility. The novel is thus an important revision of an American myth.

69 Barkhausen, Jochen. "Determining the True Color of the Chameleon: The Confusing Recovery of History in E.L. Doctorow's *Loon Lake*." See item 52.

70 Berryman, Charles. "*Ragtime* in Retrospect." *South Atlantic Quarterly* 81 (Winter 1982): 30-42.

Comments on *Ragtime*'s initial rave reviews and later dismissals, suggesting that, regardless of their evaluation, critics have missed the source of the

novel's impact. By close reading and analysis of
several episodes, Berryman shows that the novel's
strength is not its mingling of fact and fiction, but
rather in its recurring images of violence and rebirth
that suggest World War I. Compares Coalhouse
Walker's life to Scott Joplin's.

71   Bevilacqua, Winifred Farrant. "Narrating History:
       E.L. Doctorow's *The Book of Daniel.*" *Revue Française
       D´Etudes Americaines* 31 (January 1987): 53-64.
              Shows that, while this novel is a conventional
       historical one in some respects, it generally undercuts
       the assumptions of the historical novel. In part, it
       does so by blurring the distinction between fact and
       fiction, having a nondetached narrator and suggesting
       that historical understanding is subjective. Critic re-
       lates the novel's treatment of history to some work by
       historians and historiographers.

72   Bloodworth, William. "Literary Extensions of the For-
       mula Western." *Western American Literature* 14
       (Winter 1980): 287-298.
              Attempts to clarify the relationship between
       popular and literary Westerns. Believes popular West-
       erns utilize mythic notions of the West, such as its
       arid landscape, a vision of the Western hero, and a
       disjunctive sense of time and history. These mythic
       elements are also found in the literary Western. In
       Welcome to Hard Times, for example, the starkness of
       the landscape makes the attempt to form a town seem
       ludicrous. Eastern ideas of commercialism are likewise
       misplaced. Doctorow's novel inverts the Western
       hero's characteristic behavior and skews romantic
       relations. The article concludes that since literary
       Westerns draw heavily upon popular conventions,
       scholars of the literary genre should familiarize them-
       selves with the popular.

73   Bloom, Steven. "*The Book of Daniel* and the Rosen-
       berg Case, or E.L. Doctorow Meets M.R. Meeropol: A
       Dialectical Encounter Truer for Never Having Taken
       Place."
       See item 52.

74   Brienza, Susan. "Doctorow's *Ragtime*: Narratives as
       Silhouettes and Syncopations." *Dutch Quarterly
       Review of Anglo-American Letters* 11 (1981): 97-103.
              Suggests that silhouettes and ragtime music are
       the aesthetic basis of the novel. Compares the book's

sparse prose to silhouettes which the viewer must fill. Believes the novel's character and plot structure are comparable to ragtime music's syncopation and poly-rhythm. Repetition also features prominently in both this form of music and *Ragtime*.

75 ---. "The Cry of the Loon Once Heard: Patterning in Doctorow's *Loon Lake*." In item 60, 1-12.
Argues that the novel's ending is not, as some critics have claimed, out of context with the rest of the book. Article shows that throughout *Loon Lake* patterns of character doubling and role-playing sug-gest Joe will eventually imitate Bennett.

76 Busby, Mark. "E.L. Doctorow, *Ragtime* and the Dialec-tics of Change." *Ball State University Forum* 26 (Summer 1985): 39-44.
Posits that the novel is about a dialectical struggle between time's relentless progress and human desire for stability. In the novel characters who recognize the nature of the struggle fare best. Rag-time music is a fitting metaphor for the tension be-tween stability and change.

77 Campbell, Josie P. "Coalhouse Walker and the Model T Ford: Legerdemain in *Ragtime*." *Journal of Popular Culture* 13 (Fall 1979): 302-309.
States that ragtime is distinguished from most other music by its syncopation and its conflicting rhythms, and thus it provides structural and metaphorical basis for novel. Article ties this motif to Doctorow's use of Kleist's *Michael Kohlhaas*. The Coal-house Walker subplot is the insistent bass of the story, for although attention is given to all three families, a disproportionate amount goes to Coalhouse.

78 Chances, Ellen. "The Reds and *Ragtime*: The Soviet Reception of E.L. Doctorow." See item 58, 151-157.
Summarizes two major critical analyses of *Rag-time* and concludes that they represent two prevalent approaches to literary criticism in Russia. One is ex-clusively literary; the other is tied to ideology. Ar-ticle concludes that monolithic ideological criticism is no longer the kind practiced exclusively in the Soviet Union.

79 Clayton, John. "Radical Jewish Humanism: The Vision of E.L. Doctorow." See item 58, 109-120.
Claims that Doctorow writes in a tradition of

Jewish writers who deal with suffering that results from social injustice. Traces the development of strains of radicalism in Jewish-American immigrants and skepticism in Jewish thought, as well as these influences on Doctorow's work. Deals with *Welcome to Hard Times* and *The Book of Daniel.*

80 Cooper, Barbara. "The Artist as Historian in the Novels of E.L. Doctorow." *The Emporia State Research Studies* 29 (Fall 1980).
    Monograph examines *Welcome to Hard Times, Big as Life, The Book of Daniel* and *Ragtime.* Discusses how each work deals with the conflicts between subjective and objective history, and the discrepancy between people's memory of time and time itself. Argues that the artist as a historian must struggle to resolve these differences.

81 Cottrell, Robert. "The Portrayal of the American Communists in *The Book of Daniel.*" *McNeese Review* 31 (1984-1985): 64-68.
    Discusses how the novel depicts America's treatment of its Communist Party members.

82 Culp, Mildred. "Women and Tragic Destiny in Doctorow's *The Book of Daniel.*" *Studies in American Jewish Literature* 2 (1982): 155-156.
    Argues that Daniel's identity becomes known through his relatedness to female characters, and that through the female characters Doctorow suggests possible Jewish defenses in an anti-Semitic world.

83 Dawson, Anthony B. "*Ragtime* and the Movies: The Aura of the Duplicable." *Mosaic: A Journal for the Interdisciplinary Study of Literature* 16 (Winter-Spring 1983): 205-214.
    Posits that the novel's implicit linking of the Ragtime Era and the 1970s demands an aesthetic perception that began to develop with the emergence of motion pictures. The novel's prose style and motifs of duplicatability and volatility are also related to film techniques.

84 Diedrich, Maria. "E.L. Doctorow's Coalhouse Walker, Jr.: Fact in Fiction."
    See item 52.

85 Ditsky, John. "The German Source of *Ragtime*: A Note." *Ontario Review* 4 (Spring-Summer 1976): 84-86.

Cites and explains the source for the Coalhouse
Walker subplot in Kleist's story *Michael Kohlhaas.*
Then posits that using this story as a model enabled
Doctorow to underscore the unequal justice meted out
to blacks in an American period frequently viewed
nostalgically.
Also in item 58, 179–181.
See also item 121.

86   Emblidge, David. "Marching Backwards Into the
Future: Progress as Illusion in Doctorow's Novels."
Southwest Review 62 (Autumn 1977): 397–409.
Discusses *Welcome to Hard Times, The Book of
Daniel* and *Ragtime.* In each novel, history is a
repetitive process in which people are seduced as ig-
norant pawns. Each book can also be viewed as a
revenge tragedy. In *Welcome to Hard Times* Molly's
preoccupation with revenge gives the lie to Blue's
Gatsby-like search for illusory past. In *The Book of
Daniel* Daniel's obsession with revenge leads him to
historical reinterpretation. The article further discusses the importance of the raga motif (adapted from
Hindu raga music) as a commentary on the repetitive
nature of the historical process in *Ragtime,* and the
way the Coalhouse Walker subplot suggests continuing injustice in America. The critic concludes that
Doctorow is ultimately pessimistic about people's
ability to learn from the past and reform.

87   Estrin, Barbara L. "Surviving McCarthyism: E.L.
Doctorow's *The Book of Daniel.*" *Massachusetts Review:
A Quarterly of Literature, Arts and Public Affairs* 16
(Autumn-Winter 1975): 577–587.
Review article states that the novel is a reflec-
tion on the relationship between literature and politics
in the nuclear era. Discusses the novel as an in-
verted foundling story, and examines Daniel
Isaacson's long-term response to suffering.
Also in item 58, 196–206.

88   Evans, Thomas G. "Impersonal Dilemmas: The Collision
of the Modernist and Popular Tradition in Two Political
Novels, *The Grapes of Wrath* and *Ragtime.*" *South Atlantic Review* 52 (January 1987): 71–85.
Argues that *Ragtime,* like *The Grapes of Wrath,*
straddles popular and literary modernist fiction
through structures which promote both distancing and
identification, and by the use of icons. Further
argues that political novels necessarily blend popular

and high modernist art.

' 89   Faber, Marion.   "Michael Kohlhaas in New York: Kleist
        and E.L. Doctorow's *Ragtime*." In item 59, 147-156.
                Traces similarities between Kleist's tale and
        Ragtime's Coalhouse Walker episode. Focuses espe-
        cially on the use of names in *Ragtime*. Concludes that
        Doctorow makes Kleist's universal tale specific and
        eliminates the otherworldly, supernatural quality from
        coincidence. The adaptation of "Michael Kohlhaas"'s
        social aspects is nonetheless successful from a twen-
        tieth century American perspective.

90   Fogel, Stan.   "Teaching the Language of Literature."
        Dalhousie Review 59 (Autumn 1979): 527-533.
                Ends by briefly describing "False Documents" as
        a statement proposing that literature's playful lan-
        guage can be liberating.

} 91   Foley, Barbara.   "From *U.S.A.* to *Ragtime*: Notes on
        the Forms of Historical Consciousness in Modern Fic-
        tion."   *American Literature* 50 (1978): 85-105.
                Says *U.S.A.*'s crucial influence on *Ragtime* is Dos
        Passos's treatment of fact in fiction. Then argues
        that the differences between the two works are more
        important than similarities, and Doctorow's implicit
        skepticism about objective truth reflects some major
        tendencies in historically conscious fiction. *U.S.A.* is
        a watershed because it gives a microcosmic portrayal
        of a historical world in a manner characteristic of
        nineteenth-century novels. Since the time of Dos
        Passos's writing, a polarization between documentary
        and apocalyptic historical fiction has occurred. The
        critic concludes *U.S.A.* is preferable to *Ragtime* be-
        cause the former suggests hope in the material of his-
        tory itself, not in the writer's imagination.
        Also in item 58, 158-178.

92   Forrey, Robert.   "Doctorow's *The Book of Daniel*: All
        in the Family."   *Studies in American Jewish Literature*
        2 (1982): 167-173.
                Suggests that the power of *The Book of Daniel*
        springs from its Oedipal themes. Examines metaphors
        of fornication and the law as a representation of
        paternal rule.

• 93   Fremont-Smith, Eliot.   "*Ragtime* Jackpot: How to Make
        a Million Bucks in Just One Day." *Village Voice* 25
        August 1975, 35-36.

Analyzes the reasons for *Ragtime's* success, including Random House's marketing and the novel's accessible nature. Laments the market orientation of
American publishers.

* 94   Friedl, Bettina. "The Stability of Images and the In-
       stability of Things in E.L. Doctorow's *Ragtime*."
       See item 52.

* 95   Friedl, Herwig. "Power and Degradation: Patterns of
       Historical Process in the Novels of E.L. Doctorow."
       See item 52.

* 96   Gelas, Marjorie and Ruth Crowley. "Kleist in *Ragtime*:
       Doctorow's Novel, Its German Source and Its
       Reviewers." *Journal of Popular Culture* 14 (Summer
       1980): 20-26.
       Investigates why the allusion to "Michael
       Kohlhaas" was missed by the novel's reviewers. Then
       suggests that both Kleist's tale and Doctorow's novel
       hinge on the idea of constant flux in the world, but
       in *Ragtime* an awareness of perpetual instability does
       not bring terror.

97   Girgus, Sam. "In His Own Voice: E.L. Doctorow's *The
       Book of Daniel*."
       In item 52.

98   Glueck, Grace. "A Solid Gold Jubilee for Random
       House." *The New York Times* 11 August 1975, 10.
       Tells of Bantam Books' buying the paperback
       rights to *Ragtime* from Random House for $1.85 million.

99   Griffin, Bryan F. "Whoring After the New Thing: E.L.
       Doctorow and the Anxiety of Critical Reception."
       American Spectator 14 (January 1981), 7-14.
       Argues that *Loon Lake* is poorly written and
       dull, and that Doctorow's work as a whole is unin-
       teresting, as is work of Styron, Vonnegut and Coover.
       Like these other writers' novels, Doctorow's work is
       faddish and lacks serious intellectual foundation.
       These limitations reflect Doctorow's own intellectual
       limitations.

100   ------. "Panic Among the Philistines." *Harper's
       Magazine* 263 (August 1981), 37-52.
       Briefly discusses Doctorow's claims that much
       criticism of his work is ideologically based. Article on

the whole concerns the critic's view that the American literary establishment is shallow.

' 101   Gross, David. "Tales of Obscene Power: Money and Culture, Modernism and History in the Fiction of E.L. Doctorow." *Genre* 13 (1980): 71-92.

Proposes that the status of money in literature leads to the ever-scandalous discovery that people's social status determines their consciousness. Discusses literary response to money's vulgar power and posits that Doctorow's four historical novels have a typically modernist mixture of direct reference and distancing. Each, however, confronts power and money, and people's reluctance to accept them. Critic also argues that language itself is tainted like money; hence, traditional discourse cannot be used by twentieth-century protest writers.

See also "Tales of Obscene Power: Money, Culture and the Historical Fictions of E.L. Doctorow," in item 58, 120-150.

Reprinted in Male, Roy R.,ed. *Money Talks: Language and Lucre in American Fiction*. Norman, Oklahoma: University of Oklahoma Press, 1980, 71-92.

'102   ------."E.L. Doctorow." McCaffery, Larry, ed. *Postmodern Fiction: A Bio-Bibliographical Guide*. New York: Greenwood Press, 1986, 339-342.

Entry analyzes Doctorow's contribution to a kind of historical fiction that tinkers with images of the past, and thereby casts doubt on standard historical accounts.

' 103   Guillory, Daniel. "Doctorow as Poet." In item 60, 13-19.

States that Doctorow has a firm belief in the power of language and is the most poetic of the contemporary American novelists. His poetic impulse shapes a new kind of metafiction, particularly in *Loon Lake*. In this novel the inclusion of poetry apparently produced by a computer mocks people's need for verification through data.

' 104   Hague, Angela. "*Ragtime* and the Movies." *North Dakota Quarterly* 50 (Summer 1982): 101-102.

Explores the political and aesthetic implications of references to photography in this novel. Photography is seen as representing a uniquely American

way of dealing with experience and coping with a
world in constant flux.

105   Hamner, Eugenie. "The Burden of the Past:
Doctorow's *The Book of Daniel*." *Research Studies* 49
(March 1981): 55-61.
      Compares *The Book of Daniel* to Robert Penn
Warren's *All the King's Men*. Argues that through his
exploration of the case and resultant heightened
awareness of history, Daniel represents the typical
rootless, alienated person coming to terms with history.

106   Harpham, Geoffrey Galt. "E.L. Doctorow and the Technology of Narrative." *PMLA: Publications of the
Modern Language Association* 100 (January 1985): 81-
95.
      Believes Doctorow's central concern in all his
novels through *Loon Lake* is narrative. Argues that
Doctorow's narrative technique in *The Book of Daniel,
Ragtime* and *Loon Lake* reflects the dominant technology of the period which each novel portrays. From
The Book of Daniel to *Loon Lake* Doctorow moves from
a critique of the state's power, represented by the
electrical circuit; to a celebration of imaginative possibilities, represented by the computer. Critic relates
the novels' continuous redefinitions of the self to
Doctorow's resulting redefinition of the postmodernist
novel.
Also in item 60, 20-42.

✝ 107   Helbling, Robert E. "E.L. Doctorow's *Ragtime*: Kleist
Revisited." In item 59, 157-167.
      Traces similarities in plot, characterization,
philosophical outlooks and narrative objectivity in
"Michael Kohlhaas" and *Ragtime*. Differences in
Doctorow's and Kleist's prose styles are discussed.
Article focuses on the uniqueness of Michael
Kohlhaas's tale in contrast with the Coalhouse Walker
episode, which is one of many bizarre occurrences in
the novel. Concludes that "Michael Kohlhaas" is great
and powerful, while *Ragtime* is stylish.

108   Humm, Peter. "Telling Tales on the Rosenbergs."
Literature and History 12 (Spring 1986): 48-57.
      Discusses *The Book of Daniel*'s and Robert
Coover's *The Public Burning*'s rendering of the
Rosenberg case. Believes each work sees the problem
of explaining the case as a problem of narrative, but

each handles the problem differently. Coover's mythic figures and fantastic episodes remove the novel from history. In contrast, *The Book of Daniel* deals with the history of American radicalism. Furthermore, it consciously questions the process of writing history and the vulnerability of both history and fiction.

✦ 109 Hux, Samuel. "So the King Says...Says He--Historical Novel/Fictional History." *Western Humanities Review* 33 (Summer 1979): 189-201.

    Deals with the relationship between historical fiction and history, and the importance of narrative in history. Cites *Ragtime* as an extended example of how a fictional account can alter readers' perceptions of historical figures.

✦ 110 Hykisch, Anton. "E.L. Doctorow's *Ragtime*." *Slovenske Pohlady* 98 (August 1982): 122-123 (Slavic language translation).

✦ 111 Jameson, Frederic. "Post-Modernism, or the Cultural Logic of Late Capitalism." *Casa de las Americas* 155 (March-June 1986): 141-173. (in Spanish)

    In several pages, discusses *Ragtime* and *The Book of Daniel*, but focuses on *Ragtime*. Particularly notes the use of historical personages and linguistic techniques. Concludes *Ragtime* is not about history per se so much as it is about the American idea of the past.

✦ 112 Jones, Phyllis M. "*Ragtime*: Feminist, Socialist and Black Perspectives on the Self-Made Man." *Journal of American Culture* 2 (Spring 1979): 17-28.

    Argues that Doctorow depicts the three heads of households as self-made men and includes Emma Goldman in the novel in order to mock American admiration for the self-starter.

113 King, Richard H. "Between Simultaneity and
✦ Sequence."
  See item 52.

114 Knapp, Peggy A. "Hamlet and Daniel (and Freud and Marx)." *Massachusetts Review: A Quarterly of Literature, the Arts and Public Affairs* 21 (Fall 1980): 487-501.

    Discusses important similarities in the situation, psychology and attitude of Hamlet and Daniel Isaacson.

115 Knorr, Walter L. "Doctorow and Kleist: 'Kohlhaas' in
Ragtime." *Modern Fiction Studies* 22 (Summer 1976):
224-227.
Traces similarities between Coalhouse Walker
and Michael Kohlhaas. Argues that by evoking foreign
literature Doctorow creates an "anxiety of critical
reception" in readers that balances his own anxiety of
influence.

116 Krasney, Michael. "Death of the American Jewish
Novel." *MELUS: The Journal for the Study of the
Multi-Ethnic Literature of the United States.* 5
(Winter 1978): 94-97.
Contends that Jewish writers no longer write
distinctively Jewish novels and very briefly cites
Doctorow's work as a case in point.

117 Krauth, Nigel. "Fact and Fiction: The Scissors and
Paste Job." *Australian Literary Studies* 12 (1985):
119-123.
Cites *Ragtime* as an example of a contemporary
novel that uses techniques similar to those of collages.

118 Kurth, Voight and E. Liesolotte. "Kleistian Overtones
in E.L. Doctorow's *Ragtime.*" *Monatshefte: A Journal
Devoted to the Study of German Language and
Literature/fur Deutchen Utterricht, Deutsche Sprache
und Literatur* 69 (1977): 404-414.
Traces parallels in plot and characterization between Kleist's "Michael Kohlhaas" and *Ragtime.* Points
out important differences, particularly in charges
leveled against Coalhouse Walker by Booker T.
Washington as compared to those leveled against
Michael Kohlhaas by Martin Luther. Concludes that
both authors see a universal pattern of injustice and
a constant threat that any individual's life could sud-
denly become chaotic.

119 Levine, Paul. "The Conspiracy of History: E.L.
Doctorow's *The Book of Daniel.*" *Dutch Quarterly
Review of Anglo-American Letters* 11 (1981): 82-96.
States that, like all of Doctorow's historical
novels, *The Book of Daniel* is about an important turning point in American history. Argues that this novel
is not a history of the Rosenberg case but a threnody
for victims of the radical movement. *The Book of
Daniel* deals with the Isaacson children's legacy of
radicalism and with the individual's tense relationship
to society.

In item 58, 182–195.
See also item 55, 35–49.

120 ------. "E.L. Doctorow: The Writer as Survivor."
In item 52.

121 Lipecky, Heide, trans. "Coalhouse und Kohlhaas,"
Ditsky, John. *Sinn und Form* 29 (May–June 1977):
580–581.
See item 80.

122 Lorsch, Susan E. "Doctorow's *The Book of Daniel* as
Künstlerroman: The Politics of Art." *Papers on Language and Literature: A Journal for Scholars and
Critics of Languages and Literature* 18 (Winter 1982):
384–397.
By doing a close textual analysis and attending
to Biblical parallels, this article shows that *The Book
of Daniel* is a *künstlerroman* in which Daniel, through
writing his book, discovers art as a way of mediating
with society, and thus copes with the alienation
characteristic of the contemporary era.

123 Lukacs, John. "Doctorowulitzer or History in
Ragtime." *Salmagundi: A Quarterly of the Humanities
and Social Sciences Review* 31–32 (Fall 1975–Winter
1976): 285–295.
Distinguishes between the historical novel of the
nineteenth century, in which the historical events
covered were the foreground of the novel; and that of
the twentieth-century novel, in which the historical
events serve as background for individual lives. Unlike most contemporary historical novels, *Ragtime* puts
the historical events in the foreground, but it disap-
points because its real characters, such as Freud, do
things these people wouldn't. The novel is further
marred by its excessive attention to artifacts of the
period and its pictorial, rather than literary, imagination. Critic concludes that *Ragtime* suggests
Doctorow's interest in history lacks intellectual substance and, more importantly, films may have dealt a
fatal blow to literature.

124 Luzkow, Jack L. "E.L. Doctorow and the Character
Daniel: History as Fiction." In item 60, 43–52.
Believes that Daniel's analysis of the relation-
ship between American history and culture is crucial:
Daniel is unique in that as both a historian and a
participant in history he represents the tension be-

tween lived and recorded history. His marginalized
position further allows him to grasp the complexities
in American history and culture.

⌐ 125 Maryles, Daisy, ed. "Bantam Gets Ragtime for
$1,850,000, Highest Ever." *Publishers Weekly* 207
(11 August 1975): 55-56.
    Tells of Bantam getting the reprint rights to
Ragtime at record-breaking price.

126 ------. "Ragtime: Bantam Unveils Its Offbeat Marketing Plans." *Publishers Weekly* 209 (26 April 1976): 45-
46.
    Describes Bantam's innovative marketing plan,
including displays, cassettes and teachers' guides, for
Ragtime.

• 127 Matheson, William. "Doctorow's *Ragtime*." *Explicator*
42 (Winter 1984): 21-22.
    Cites several references to "rags" in novel, and
concludes that the title suggests the economic ineq-
uity of the time, as well as ragtime music.

128 McGrath, Peter. "The Debate That Will Not Die."
Newsweek 31 October, 1983, 94.
    Discusses the controversy over the Rosenberg
case in the light of the American Left's historical
relationship with the Communist Party. Briefly refers
to *The Book of Daniel* and the movie *Daniel*.

129 Mitgang, Herbert. "A Novel from E. L. Doctorow."
The New York Times 5 September 1980, C20.
    Reports that *Loon Lake* is forthcoming; and
briefly discusses Doctorow's novels, the reception of
their political content and Doctorow's professional ac-
tivities.

130 Nadel, Alan. "Hero and Other in Doctorow's *Loon
Lake*." *College Literature* 14 (Spring 1987): 136-146.
    Argues that, unlike *The Book of Daniel* and
Ragtime, which present history as a discourse created
by the tension between notoriety and otherness, *Loon
Lake* investigates the process by which one makes the
leap from otherness to history. The article draws
upon Wordsworthian notions of writing and sees the
influence of Nabokov's *Pale Fire*.

• 131 Neumeyer, Peter F. "E.L. Doctorow, Kleist and the As-
cendancy of Things." *CEA Critic: An Official Journal*

of the College English Association 39 (May 1977): 17–
21.

Contrasts *Ragtime* with earlier American fiction
(even Doctorow's own *The Book of Daniel*) and with
"Michael Kohlhaas." Contends that in earlier fiction
writers tried to express compelling truths by concentrating on individual characters, and that Michael
Kohlhaas himself is a victim of his fierce individuality.
Ragtime, however, portrays a world in which
individuals are unimportant unless they manufacture
things.

132 "1975, the Best Sellers." *Publishers Weekly* 209 (9
February 1976): 42.

Says *Ragtime* is somewhat unusual in that the
author's name is new to the Annual Best-Seller List.
States that 232,340 copies have been sold and the
book has won the National Book Critics Circle Fiction
Award and set a record in paperback reprint rights.

133 Olderman, Raymond. "American Fiction 1974–1976—
People Who Fell to Earth." *Contemporary Literature*
19 (Autumn 1978): 497–530.

Briefly comments on *Ragtime* in bibliographic
essay on the thematic concerns and stylistic features
of American fiction written in stated years.

ι134 Piehl, Kathy. "E.L. Doctorow and Random House: The
Ragtime Rhythm of Cash." *Journal of Popular Culture*
13 (Winter 1979): 404–411.

Reports on Random House's aggressive promotion of the hardcover edition of the book, the
hardcover's commercial success and the paperback's
poor showing.

135 Pierce, Constance. "The Syncopated Voices in
Doctorow's *Ragtime*." *Notes on Modern American
Literature* 3 (Fall 1979): Item 26.

Suggests that the narrator gains his authority
through his surrealistic view of history. The boy's
speaking in the first person suggests readers have no
access to history other than through the perceptions
of various chroniclers. Critic sees *Ragtime* as a self-
reflexive novel.

136 Pincherskĭ, Mar. "Summa istoria: Notaatky perek-
ladacha." *Vsevit: Literaturno-Mystetskyi ta Hromods
ko-Politychnyĭ Zhurnal* 2 (February 1982): 147–149.

Articles

137   Rapf, Joanna. "'Some Fantasy on Earth': Doctorow's
      Welcome to Hard Times." *Literature/Film Quarterly* 13
      (1985): 50-55.
          Argues that although filmmakers may be free to
      reshape novels' inherent values by ironic commentary,
      Burt Kennedy's "Welcome to Hard Times" radically dis-
      torts the deep pessimism of Doctorow's novel.

❙138 Reitz, Bernhard. "A Society of Ragamuffins--
      Fortschritt und Fiktion in E.L. Doctorow's *Ragtime.*"
      Anglistik und Englischunterricht 24 (1984): 135-154.
          Contends *Ragtime* is often misunderstood and
      probes the reasons why. After initial rave reviews, a
      a second wave of critics judged the novel harshly be-
      cause they were measuring it against the traditional
      historical novel. *Ragtime* is a different kind of histori-
      cal novel that suggests our concept of history is illu-
      sion. (in German)

❢ 139 Rodgers, Bernard F. "A Novelist's Revenge: *Ragtime.*"
      Chicago Review 27 (Winter 1975): 138-144.
          Examines the qualities of *Ragtime* that made it
      both a critical and a popular success. Posits that its
      popular appeal is in the story of three diverse
      families and its critical appeal is rooted in its complex
      metaphor of ragtime music.

❢140 Saltzman, Arthur. "The Stylistic Energy of E.L. Doc-
      torow."   In item 58, 73-108.
          Maintains that Doctorow is unique among
      postmodernist writers because he is both socially con-
      scious and stylistically innovative. Traces the
      relationship between style, imagery and content in
      *Welcome to Hard Times, Big as Life, The Book of
      Daniel, Ragtime* and *Loon Lake.* Argues that Doctorow
      attempts to demythologize his own craft and dismantle
      American myths.

⸲ 141 Schulz, Dieter. "E.L. Doctorow's America: An Intro-
      duction to His Fiction." See item 52.

142   Shelton, Frank W. "E.L. Doctorow's *Welcome to Hard
      Times:* The Western and the American Dream." *Mid-
      west Quarterly: A Journal of Contemporary Thought*
      25 (Autumn 1983): 7-17.
          Says this novel deserves serious consideration
      because, in addition to being an outstanding work, it
      contains the seeds of Doctorow's views on the role of
      history and fate in human lives. Implies that

Doctorow uses the popular Western genre to suggest the empty promise of the American Dream.

143 Shiels, Michael. "'Look! It's James Cagney':
Strategies of Cinematic Fictionalization in Milos
Forman's *Ragtime.*" In item 52.

144 Smith, Duncan. "'Michael Kohlhaas' and *Ragtime*: The
Hopeful Text and the Despairing Story." *Wis-
senschaftliche Zeitschrift der Wilhelm-Pieck* Univer-
sitat Rostock. Gessellschrafts- und Sprachwis-
senschaftliche Reihe 31 (1982): 3-7.

145 Stark, John. "Alienation and Analysis in Doctorow's
The Book of Daniel." *Critique: Studies in Modern
Fiction* 16, 3 (1975): 101-110.
Examines the concepts of alienation and
analysis by focusing on the novel's images. Concludes
Doctorow's major point is that an analyst should con-
centrate on images, and by doing so he/she can
decrease alienation.

146 Steinberg, Cobbett. "History and the Novel:
Doctorow's *Ragtime.*" *University of Denver Quarterly*
10 (Winter 1976): 125-130.
Review essay expresses concern about the
apolitical, asocial nature of 1960s American fiction.
Summarizes the novel's historical relationship to
veracity and examines *The Book of Daniel* as a work
that is both politically relevant and artistically
accomplished. Concludes that *Ragtime* is likewise an
effective blend of accomplished writing and relevant
social themes.

147 Stern, Richard. "Penned In." *Critical Inquiry* 13
(Autumn 1980): 1-32.
Gives a brief account of Doctorow's objections
to Schultz's address at the 1986 PEN Conference.
Part of an overview article on the conference.
See item 33.

148 Strout, Cushing. "Radical Religion and the American
Political Novel. "*Clio: An Interdisciplinary Journal of
Literature, History & the Philosophy of History* 6
(Fall 1976): 23-42.
See item 57.

149 ------. "Historicizing Fiction and Fictionalizing
History: The Case of E.L. Doctorow." *Prospects: An*

Annual Journal of American Cultural Studies 5 (1980): 423-437.

Examines Doctorow's work in the context of structuralist and recent historical theory. Argues that while *The Book of Daniel* is true to the historical Rosenberg case and powerful because of this verisimilitude, *Ragtime* manipulates history irresponsibly and for thinly veiled political purposes.

150 ------. "Reconsidering the Rosenbergs: History, Novel, Film." *Reviews in American History* 12 (September 1984): 309-321.

Gives an overview of essays that have covered the Rosenberg case and then discusses *The Book of Daniel*, the film *Daniel* (item 480), and *The Rosenberg File* by Ronald Radosh (item 527). Concludes that the novel admirably renders many of the case's complexities, but the film rendition is much simpler and is likely to be viewed as a statement of the couple's innocence. *The Rosenberg File*, although weak in dealing with the defendants' psychology, has the outstanding strength of fairly considering material on both sides.

151 Tanner, Stephen L. "Rage and Order in Doctorow's *Welcome to Hard Times*." *South Dakota Review* 22 (Autumn 1984): 79-85.

Argues that *Welcome to Hard Times* is a flawed attempt to invert the Western genre in which order is first destroyed and then restored. Doctorow's novel is marred by the underlying pop psychology implicit in its themes of Oedipal conflict and death wish. More importantly, the novel is undercut by Doctorow's insufficient knowledge of the psychology of living in the West.

152 Tokarczyk, Michelle M. "From the Lions' Den: Survivors in E.L. Doctorow's *The Book of Daniel*." *Critique: Studies in Modern Fiction* 29 (Fall 1987): 3-15.

Shows that the Isaacson children and Linda Mindish have psychological traits of survivors of political persecution. Argues that such characterizations allow Doctorow to imply that the abuses of the McCarthy era have left permanent scars and cannot, as some Americans hope, be swept away by the progressivism of subsequent decades.
Adapted from item 164, 122-157.

153   Turner, Joseph W. "The Kinds of Historical Fiction:
An Essay in Definition and Methodology." *Genre* 12
(Fall 1979): 333-355.
    Defines three different kinds of historical
fiction: those that invent the past, those that disguise
the documented past and those that recreate the
documented past. Suggests that *The Book of Daniel* is
problematic because it generates expectations of
documentary fiction while apparently being a completely fictive work.

154   Versluys, Kristiaan. "E.L. Doctorow's Recent Work:
Tales of the Struggling Self." *Spieghel Historiael* 28
(1986-1987): 78-86.
    Argues that Doctorow's recent quasi-
autobiographical work, *Lives of the Poets: A Novella
and Six Short Shories* and *World's Fair*, ponder how
life should be lived. Often the characters are faced
with extreme choices, and the successful ones balance
alternatives.

155   ------. "E.L. Doctorow: The Struggle Against Evil."
Versluys, ed. *Recent Trends in American Writing:
Proceedings of the Belgiam Luxembourg American
Studies Association Conference.* Ghent: 1987, 55-72.
    Focuses on *Welcome to Hard Times* and *The
Book of Daniel* as Doctorow's first important books
which suggest the important themes in all his later
work. Then covers four essential points in discussing
Doctorow's work: its American quality, its postmodern
historicism, its stylistic innovation, and, most impor-
tant and frequently ignored, its grappling with
psychological and philosophical problems.
See item 56.

* 156   Winkler, Allan M. "*Ragtime* and the United States
before World War I."
See item 52.

*157   Wüstenhagen, Heinz. "Edgar L. Doctorow's *Ragtime*:
*Weimarer Beiträge: Zeitschrift für Literaturwis-
senschraft, Ästhetik und Kulturtheorie* 31 (1985):
452-465.
    Discusses *Ragtime* in the context of the
development of the historical novel in the United
States. Critic believes that the title of this novel
suggests its age's cultural signature, including its
tensions and contradictions. The use of Kleist's
"Michael Kohlhaas" in particular indicates an aware-

ness of growing class and racial inequality. Article concludes that Doctorow and many of his contemporaries use history to explain the present national identity. (in German)

158   Zins, Daniel L.   "Daniel's 'Teacher' in Doctorow's *The Book of Daniel.*"   *Notes on Modern American Literature* 3 (Spring 1979): Item 16.
      Suggests that Daniel as a graduate student ostensibly writing a dissertation about his parents' case is indebted to the revisionist historian William Appleman Williams for the political analysis of America's foreign policy and ultimately for the insights gained through self-analysis.

159   ------.   "E.L. Doctorow: The Novelist as Historian." *The Hollins Critic* 16 (1979): 1-14.
      Analyzes the way that *Welcome to Hard Times*, *The Book of Daniel*, and *Ragtime* are revisionist historical novels ultimately implying that if Americans are not willing to analyze some of their worst mistakes, they may become passive victims of their own history.

160   ------.   "Doctorow's Theater of Ideas."   *Southwest Review*   66 (Winter 1981): 96-100.
      Discusses the plot of *Drinks Before Dinner* in the context of Doctorow's concept of "theater of ideas," in which ideas are seen as part of a struggle for survival.   Suggests this concept is not typically American.   Concedes the play has been received poorly by reviewers, but urges a reconsideration.

161   ------.   "Teaching English in a Nuclear Age."   *College English* 47 (April 1985): 387-406.
      Discusses *The Book of Daniel* and Robert Coover's *The Public Burning* as two novels whose adaptations of the Rosenberg case brilliantly demonstrate the pernicious nature of America's belief that there were atomic secrets.   Advocates these books as part of a curriculum that could be used to educate students about the dangers of nuclear war.

G
DISSERTATIONS

162　Boyer, Eric Russell. "Reading *Ragtime*: A Postmodern American Economic Novel." Syracuse University: Syracuse, New York, August 1984.

　　　Uses a reader-response approach to show how readers can benefit from a transgressive reading of the novel that opens up diverse possibilities. Applies his theories about this novel to the teaching of composition classes.

163　Powell, Jerry Owen. "The Case as History, Fiction and Myth--1970s." In item 554, 206-219.

　　　Structuralist approach utilized in this chapter analyzes the benefits of Doctorow's making Daniel the writer of the account in *The Book of Daniel*. Sees Daniel's skepticism, the novel's shifts in tone, its sudden shifts in content and the numerous plausible interpretations of the Rosenberg case as discouraging simple interpretations by readers. Concludes that Doctorow is ultimately skeptical about the worth of historical analysis, particularly sequential cause-and-effect analysis.

164　Tokarczyk, Michelle M. "The Rosenberg Case and E.L. Doctorow's *The Book of Daniel*: A Study of the Use of History in Fiction." SUNY at Stony Brook, Stony Brook, New York: May 1985.

　　　Examines the major themes in *The Book of Daniel* and Doctorow's other work from *Welcome to Hard Times* through *Loon Lake*. Argues that the historical Rosenberg case inspired an innovative treatment of literary, historical and psychological ideas, and spurred Doctorow to become an experimental novelist. A New Historical approach is utilized. This is the first dissertation exclusively on Doctorow's work.

165　Zins, Daniel L. "A Failure of Analysis: Mass Hysteria and Its Legacy," in "Cuckoo's Nest and Joe McCarthy:

Sanity and Madness in Contemporary Fiction." Emory
University, Atlanta, Georgia: May 1979, 112-163.
  Discusses how the Isaacson children are
depicted as insane. Then by drawing on the work of
psychologists Carl Jung and R.D. Laing, and examining
American post-World War II nuclear policy and the
character of the McCarthy era, argues that mass men-
tal illness is no different from the individual variety.

H
INTERVIEWS

166   Baker, John F. "PW Interviews: E.L. Doctorow." *Publishers Weekly* 207 (30 June 1975): 6-7.
     Covers the genesis of *Ragtime*, its mingling of fact and fiction, Doctorow's current writing and his publishing career. Contains Doctorow's often quoted remark that *Ragtime* is a "novelist's revenge" in an era that values nonfiction.

167   Belza, Sviatoslav. "Mify Obschchestva." *Literaturnaia Gazeta* 39 (24 September 1986): 15.

168   Domeny, Katalin. Interview for *Mozgò Vilag*, in press. (in Hungarian).

169   Friedl, Herwig and Dieter Schulz. "A Multiplicity of Witness: E.L. Doctorow at Heidelberg."
     See item 52.

170   Gussow, Mel. "Novelist Syncopates History in *Ragtime*." *The New York Times* 11 July 1975, 12.
     Gives history of how *Ragtime* evolved. Then sums up Doctorow's views on the relationship between fact and fiction, and his hopes that working class people will read this accessible novel. Also cites Doctorow's view that social scientists have appropriated cultural stories, leaving novelists with a constricted domain of personal experience.

171   Levine, Paul. "The Writer as Independent Witness." In item 58, 57-69.
     Focuses on Doctorow's perception of America. Suggests America has little sense of history and historical novels can ameliorate this by fostering a sense of community. Maintains that American writers have always been political, but their treatment in universities has been apolitical. Then discusses *The Book of*

Daniel as a novel about the sacrificial role of the Left and about inheritance. Posits that America is politically naive and links this naivete to a national pragmatic reliance upon technology. Doctorow asserts that the writer, untied to any system or institution, can act as an independent witness and affirm the plurality in American culture and politics rather than assert any particular truth.

Also Canadian Broadcasting Company, radio series "Ideas," March 1978.

⌐172   Lubarsky, Jared. "History and the Forms of Fiction: An Interview With E.L. Doctorow." *Eigo Seinen* 124, 4 (1978): 150-152.
   Covers the relationship between writers and editors in America, the relationship between history and fiction, Doctorow's inspiration for several novels, and the theme of the individual against society in modern fiction.

ᶠ173   McCaffery, Larry. "A Spirit of Transgression." In *Anything Can Happen: Interviews With Contemporary Novelists* by Tom Le Clair and Larry McCaffery University of Illinois Press: Urbana, Chicago and London, 1983, 91-105.
   Focuses on Doctorow's career and evolution as writer, dealing with *Welcome to Hard Times*, *The Book of Daniel*, *Ragtime*, and *Loon Lake*. The influence of Doctorow's undergraduate education in philosophy is discussed. Doctorow maintains that his art is not a product of preconceived notions and that each novel evolves differently. He then discusses his treatment of history and his view that all history is composed. Also in item 58, 31-47.

174   McInerney, James. "Author, Author: An Interview with Doctorow." *Vogue* 174 (November 1984), 152-155.
   Briefly recaps Doctorow's life and discusses *Lives of the Poets* as a book about contemporary writers and the isolated nature of modern society.

⤵175   Mills, Hillary. "Creators on Creating: E.L. Doctorow." *Saturday Review: A Review of Literature and the Creative Arts*   7 (October 1980), 44-48.
   Explores Doctorow's inspirations for writing, work practices and political and social outlooks.

⤵176   Navasky, Victor S. "E.L. Doctorow: I Saw a Sign." *The New York Times Book Review*,   28 September 1980, 44-45.

Discusses Doctorow's attitude toward inspiration, narrative technique and political themes in novels.

177   O'Neill, Catherine. "The Music in Doctorow's Head." *Books & Arts*, 28 September 1979, 5.
Discusses the critical reception of *Drinks Before Dinner* and Doctorow's general views on contemporary American theater. Doctorow states he believes the critics panned his play because it was a drama of ideas, and most current theater is sadly lacking in substance. Interview then gives brief overview of Doctorow's life and work.

ˋ178   Plimpton, George. "The Art of Fiction." *The Paris Review* 28 (Winter 1986): 23-47.
Focuses on Doctorow's creative process and opinions as to what a writer needs and what aids the composing process. *World's Fair, Lives of the Poets: A Novella and Six Short Stories, The Book of Daniel, Loon Lake, Ragtime* and *Drinks Before Dinner* are discussed. This printed interview is taken from an interview conducted in public and includes questions from the audience.

ˋ179   "*Ragtime* Revisited: A Seminar with E.L. Doctorow and Joseph Papaleo." *Nieman Reports* 31 (Summer/Autumn 1977):   3+.
Transcript of a Nieman Seminar consisting of Doctorow's and Papaleo's conversations with others. Writers are questioned about the relationship between fiction and history, and Doctorow states that for the novelist history is a source of images. He further maintains that a writer can bear witness to events by fictionalizing them because fiction can sensitize people.

180   Rinzler, Carol E. "A Dialogue With Doctorow." *Cosmopolitan* 199 (November 1985), 66.
Probes *World's Fair's* genesis, narrative technique and possible autobiographical content.

ˋ181   Sanoff, Alvin P. "A Conversation with E.L. Doctorow: Writing is Often a Desperate Act." *U.S. News and World Report* 99 (16 December 1985), 73-74.
Discusses Doctorow's view that the creative process is often accidental. Also focuses on the nature of the contemporary American novel and *World's Fair* as a novel about a child's perceptions.

ˋ182   Schillinger, Liesl. "E.L. Doctorow: A Talk." *The Yale*

Vernacular 1 (March/April 1987): 10-13.
Gives an overview of Doctorow's views on the
nature of writing in contemporary America, the content and some important themes in his work and the
films based on his books. Also touches on Doctorow's
opinions on feminism.

* 183 Trenner, Richard. "Politics and the Mode of Fiction."
*The Ontario Review: North American Journal of the
Arts* 16 (Spring-Summer 1982): 5-16.
Focuses on Doctorow's political beliefs and the
way they influence his writing. Explores Doctorow's
family's political orientation. Probes whether there is
a Jewish tradition of questing for justice and in the
course of the discussion Doctorow gives his own
definition of justice. His ideas are placed in the context of the Constitution's importance to American justice.
Also in item 58, 48-56.

184 Weber, Bruce. "The Myth Maker: The Creative Mind of
Novelist E.L. Doctorow." *The New York Times
Magazine,* 20 October 1985, 24+.
Gives a brief biography and discusses the
themes in Doctorow's work, positing that each novel
deals with "the evolution of the American perspective." The soon-to-be-released *World's Fair* is particularly noted, and an excerpt of the novel is included.

See also *Dialogue* 74 (Fall 1986): 57+.

*185 Yardley, Jonathan. "Mr. Ragtime." *The Miami Herald*
21 December 1975, 1K, 3K.
Deals with Doctorow's views on the upcoming
film based on *Ragtime,* as well as gives his views on
the relationship between literature and film. Doctorow
asserts that novelists must grapple with modern
technology's having made people's minds more visual
and fast-paced. Interview also provides biographical
information.

⸱186 Ackroyd, Peter. "TV Times." *Spectator* 236 (24
      January 1976), 25.
          Says *Ragtime*'s techniques have all been used
      previously with greater success. Finds novel nothing
      more than a "comic book version" of American culture,
      a sentimental work lacking in plot and character
      development. Posits that American reviewers liked
      Ragtime because it has the guise of being about
      American history and culture.

187   Adams, Phoebe. Short Reviews: Books. *Atlantic
      Monthly* 236 (July 1975), 88.
          One paragraph review calls *Ragtime* an excep-
      tionally original and pleasurable novel.

188   Allen, Bruce. "It Was a Very Good Year: Doctorow's
      Lives of the Poets." *The Christian Science Monitor*
      77 (4 January 1985), B2.
          Describes the book as the year's best work of
      fiction. Praises the sharp phrasing and precise im-
      agery in the book which is ultimately about a writer's
      progression from psychological confusion to human
      connectedness.

189   Atwood, Margaret. "E.L. Doctorow: Writing by His Own
      Rules." *Book World* 10 (28 September 1980), 1-2, 10.
          Discusses *Loon Lake* in the context of *Ragtime*'s
      success and the effect of such successes on novelists.
      Finds period detail in *Loon Lake* accurate and some
      sections of the novel beautifully written. Admires the
      treatment of the dark side of the American Dream, but
      believes the novel is not coherent, and the ending
      particularly fails.

      Reprinted in Atwood, Margaret. *Second Words:*

Selected Critical Prose. Toronto: House of Anasi
Press, Ltd., 1982, 325-328.

190   Autrand, Dominique. "Un Best Seller Que Mêle L'Historie a la Fiction Avec Une Vitalie Suprenante." La
Quinzaine Litteraire 16 (31 October 1976): 11-12.
      Recounts the major events of Ragtime and
praises it as an outstanding American historical novel.

191   Balliett, Whitney. "Through History with E.L.
Doctorow." The New Yorker 56 (8 December 1980),
232-234.
      Contends that Doctorow's work on the whole is
weak and that he chooses prose styles ill-suited to
the historical periods he depicts. Finds that Loon
Lake poorly imitates the styles of Dos Passos,
Faulkner, Joyce and Stein. Furthermore, its plot is
thin and predictable.

192   ------. "Mel-O-Rols, Knickers, and Gee Bee Racers."
The New Yorker 61 (9 December 1985), 153+.
      States that World's Fair is a fragment of a novel
that includes little more than memorabilia of 1930s.
The actual novel does not begin until the book is two-
thirds finished.

193   Bannon, Barbara A. Forecasts. Publishers Weekly
191 (6 March 1967): 78.
      Praises Welcome to Hard Times as a nondidactic
parable depicting war between good and evil.

194   ------. PW Forecasts. Publishers Weekly 207 (26
May 1975): 53.
      Praises Ragtime for its plot and its effective
treatment of the dangerous undercurrents in America's
ragtime era. Calls the novel a "satiric melodrama."

195   ------. PW Forecasts. Publishers Weekly 218 (8
August 1980): 76.
      Claims Loon Lake is a splendid achievement be-
cause it is both a tantalizing story and a part of
Doctorow's ongoing work on how the American character evolved. Review summarized in item 307.

196   Barber, Michael. Paperbacks. Books 2 (May 1987), 33.
      One-paragraph review calls World's Fair an
elegiac autobiography that conveys America's sense of
optimism in the midst of the Depression.

197   Bawer, Bruce. "The Human Dimension." *Nation* 239
      (17 November 1984), 515-519.
            Reviews *Lives of the Poets: A Novella and Six
      Short Stories* and gives an overview of Doctorow's
      work to date. Faults all Doctorow's work for its lack
      of character development and its didactic treatment of
      the American Dream. Criticizes the novella *Lives of
      the Poets* in particular for its unrealistic characteriza-
      tion and contrived ending. Finds the other stories in
      this collection similarly flawed.

198   Beards, Richard A. Review of *Lives of the Poets: A
      Novella and Six Short Stories. World Literature
      Today: A Literary Quarterly of the University of
      Oklahoma* 59 (Summer 1985): 427-428.
            Says the collection challenges readers to com-
      pose a picture of the writer from his varied works,
      but the novella meant to unify these works does not
      because it lapses into cliche portrayals of midlife
      crises.

199   Bell, Pearl K. "Guilt on Trial." *New Leader: A Bi-
      Weekly of News and Opinion* 54 (28 June 1971), 17-19.
            Reviews *The Book of Daniel* with Mordechai
      Richler's *St. Urbain's Horseman*. Believes *The Book of
      Daniel* is an ambitious failure because Doctorow's
      stylistic innovations are confusing rather than effec-
      tive and because the novel does not confront the
      issue of the Rosenbergs' guilt.

200   ------. "Singing the Same Old Song." *Commentary* 70
      (October 1980), 70-73.
            Loon Lake is one of several novels reviewed.
      Reviewer criticizes Doctorow's book as having a thin
      story line, being stylistically poor and a weak imita-
      tion of Dos Passos' *USA*. Concludes Doctorow's im-
      agination is constrained by his simpleminded left-wing
      dogma.

·201 "Birth of the Blues." *Economist* 258 (24 January
      1976), 108.
            Praises *Ragtime* as one of the best American
      novels in years. Sees this book as depicting a crucial
      period in the development of the American Dream in
      its best and worst aspects, while giving just attention
      to the tragedies of the families involved. Also praises
      the book's graceful style.

202 Blakeston, Oswell. Fiction   Books and Bookmen 17
     (April 1972): 50.
          Reviews *The Book of Daniel* and two other
     novels. Sees *The Book of Daniel* as a work full of
     indignation, but sufficiently well-crafted to keep
     readers engrossed.

203 Blue, Adrienne. "The Real Shock." *New Statesman: An
     Independent Political and Literary Review* 109 (5 April
     1985), 32-33.
          *Lives of the Poets: A Novella and Six Short
     Stories* is one of several books reviewed. One
     paragraph calls Doctorow an accomplished exurban
     writer and discusses the father-son relationship in
     "The Writer in the Family."

204 Bluestein, Gene. "Moral Dilemma." *Progressive* 44
     (December 1980), 59-61.
          Believes that although *The Book of Daniel* and
     Ragtime were powerful, well-written books, *Loon Lake*
     fails in every respect. Its experimental prose lacks
     daring and beauty; its ending is unconvincing.

205 ------. "Time Capsule." *Progressive* 50 (March
     1986), 42-43.
          Praises *World's Fair* as a superb work of fiction
     that reconstructs a boy's life and the artifacts of the
     1930s that give the period its signature.

206 Book Briefs. *Business Week* (6 October 1980), 15.
          One-paragraph review describes *Loon Lake* as
     an interesting attempt to blend disparate voices: one
     telling of the hopelessness of the Depression, the
     other celebrating the pastoral beauty of the Adiron-
     dacks. Concludes that this admirable, innovative at-
     tempt largely fails, however.

207 "*Book World* Picks Fifty Notable Books of 1971." *Book
     World* 5 (5 December 1971): 5.
          Capsule review of *The Book of Daniel* describes
     it as an excellent book about politics that exposes the
     dreams and flaws of the American Communist Party.

᠈ 208 Bradbury, Malcolm. "The *Ragtime* Bandwagon." *Punch*
     270 (21 January 1976), 136-137.
          Praises *Ragtime* for its use of ragtime rhythms
     in prose and for its exposition of the illusion of his-
     tory in a period piece.

209 Bragg, Melvin. *Illustrated London News* 265, May 1977, 87.

Ragtime is one of ten books reviewed. Review praises Doctorow's novel as a particularly American accomplishment. Is impressed by its blend of historical fact and fiction, its expansive scope and readable prose.

210 Briefly Noted. In *The New Yorker* 51 (28 July 1975), 79–80.

Praises *Ragtime*'s richness, although the reviewer wishes Doctorow looked more deeply into characters.

211 Brownjohn, Allan. "Breaking the Rules." *Encounter* 5 (May 1981), 86–91.

Discusses *Loon Lake* and several other books. Finds the narrative and depiction of the historical period better than they were in *Ragtime*. Praises Doctorow's skill in interweaving Joe's and Penfield's stories.

212 Burgess, Anthony. "Doctorow's 'Hit' is a Miss." *Saturday Review: A Review of Literature and the Creative Arts* 7 (September 1980), 66–67.

States that with its combination of technical innovation and traditional novelistic properties (such as character development) *Loon Lake* breaks new ground. Although the novel isn't successful, its failures are the kind that signal a promising writer.

213 Catinella, Joseph. Review of *The Book of Daniel*. In *Saturday Review: A Review of Literature and the Creative Arts* 54 (17 July 1971), 32, 61.

Praises Doctorow as a novelist who seriously and confidently confronts political issues, but believes the couple's personal tragedy is often minimized by the novel's experimental prose.

214 Caute, David. Review of *The Book of Daniel*. In *Guardian Weekly* 106 (26 February 1972), 18.

Sees the novel as a stunning masterpiece and rates Doctorow a better contemporary political novelist than any but Solzhenitsyn. Faults novel's depiction of prosecution's chief witness as friend rather than relative.

215 Charyn, Jerome. "Deprived of the Right to be Dangerous." *The New York Times Book Review*, 4 July 1971, 6.

Believes *The Book of Daniel* is most powerful in depicting the Isaacson family and recreating the Cold War climate of the 1950s. The novel is flat when depicting 1960s New Left politics.

216 Chevigny, Bell Gale. "Orphans by Electrocution." *Village Voice*, 9 September 1971, 19.

Describes *The Book of Daniel* as a novel about the burden of being orphans, the Cold War climate in America and the search for continuity between the Old and New Left. Concludes *The Book of Daniel* is provocative because it refuses to provide definitive interpretations and forces its readers to do so.

217 Clemons, Walter. "Houdini, Meet Ferdinand." *Newsweek* 86 (14 July 1975), 73, 76.

Commends *Ragtime*'s grace, lively prose and episodes. Believes this novel explores the American Dream and the American character in general. Includes a brief biography and discussion of Doctorow's views on the distinction between fiction and nonfiction.

218 ------. "In the Shadow of the War." *Newsweek* 106 (4 November 1985), 69.

Finds *World's Fair* tedious and bogged down in detail, more like a memoir than a novel. Implicitly questions if Doctorow's blurring of genres works here and if autobiographical writing is one of Doctorow's strengths.

219 Coleby, John. "Plays in Print." *Drama: The Quarterly Theatre Review* 135 (January 1980): 74–75.

States that although the produced play had a stunning cast and intended to highlight the maladies of contemporary life, *Drinks Before Dinner* has little strength besides its sense of heightened language.

220 Core, George. "Read 'Em Cowboy." *The American Scholar* 50 (Summer 1981): 389–400.

Welcome to Hard Times is one of twelve books reviewed. Review looks at the power of the Western myth and its current popularity in the United States. Calls Doctorow's novel a powerful allegory of good and evil. Concludes writers such as Doctorow make readers realize the complexity of the American West's fate.

221 Crowley, John W. Review of *Loon Lake*. In *America* 145 (12 September 1981), 124.
Praises the novel's power, which derives from Doctorow's embracing opposites such as realism and aestheticism.

222 Cunliffe, Marcus. "Material for Every Appetite." *Manchester Guardian Weekly* 114 (1 February 1976), 22.
Praises *Ragtime* for being an artful, imaginative rendition of the past. Believes some aspect of this novel will appeal to almost every reader.

223 Curran, Ronald. Review of *Loon Lake*. In *World Literature Today: A Literary Quarterly of the University of Oklahoma* 55 (Summer 1981): 472.
Describes the novel as ambitious in a Faulknerian sense, but thinks its themes and character sketches require clarification.

224 Davies, Russell. "Mingle With the Mighty." *Times Literary Supplement*, 23 January 1976, 77.
Sees *Ragtime* as little more than a set of caricatures presented in prose that is at times wooden, at times inflated. Posits that Americans, who still need to debunk heroes, are delighted by irreverent treatment of notables.

225 De Mott, Benjamin. "Doctorow's Promise." *Atlantic Monthly* 246 (September 1980), 105-107.
Says *Loon Lake* has more detailed characterizations than *Ragtime*, but is still lacking because its characters suggest discomfort with emotional attachment. Concludes that *Loon Lake* could be Doctorow's first step in engaging his readers with more substantial literature which explores peoples' emotions: Thus *Loon Lake* holds genuine promise.

226 ------. "Pilgrim Among the Culturati." *The New York Times Book Review*, 11 November 1984, 1, 35-36.
Summarizes the plot of the stories and the novella in *Lives of the Poet: A Novella and Six Short Stories*. Suggests that the novella gives form to the seemingly miscellaneous collection and helps readers to see the novella's hero as a pilgrim for truth. Though somewhat troubled by the novella's self-reflexiveness,

the reviewer finds merit in its implicit struggle for
meaning.

227 Doherty, Gail and Paul. Book Reviews: Softcover
Selections for Seventy-Seven Literature. *America* 136
(29 January 1977), 81.
    Recommends *Ragtime* as one of the ten best
novels recently published in paperback. Brief summary describes the book as an adventure story that
inverts conventional uses of nostalgia.

228 Dollen, Charles. Review of *Ragtime*. In *Best Sellers*
35 (September 1975): 150.
    Says the book is deliberately and charmingly
Victorian, should be popular, and definitely has movie
possibilities.

229 Donald, Miles. "Bad on Paper." *New Statesman: An
Independent Political and Literary Review* 83 (18
February 1972), 216.
    The Book of Daniel is one of five books
reviewed. Its theme of a search for identity is too
thin for a novel; on the whole the book is dull and
important questions are left unanswered.

230 Duffy, Martha. "Into the Night." *Time* 98 (19 July
1971), 74
    Reviews *The Book of Daniel* with *A Peep Into the
Twentieth Century* by Christopher Davis. States that
Doctorow's novel succeeds through its energy and
drama, and through its wise focus on the emotions of
the Atom Spy couple's children rather than on political issues.

231 du Plessix Gray, Francine. "Critics' Choice for
Christmas." *Commonweal* 107 (5 December 1980), 696.
    Loon Lake is one of four books reviewed. The
novel is praised for its blend of lyricism and political
themes. It is also described as Doctorow's first
romantic novel.

232 Eder, Richard. Review of *World's Fair*. In *Los
Angeles Times Book Review*, 24 November 1985, 3.
    Believes Doctorow's novel of a writer's boyhood
lacks the genius of Joyce's *A Portrait of the Artist* as
a Young Man, but is successful in rendering details
and depicting how an artist's sensibility is shaped.

233 Emerson, Sally. "Recent Fiction: Family and Love."
Illustrated London News 274 (February 1986), 68.
Reviews *World's Fair* and two other books. In
one paragraph describes Doctorow's novel as well-
written, but without a clear narrative thread.

234 Erler, Mary C. Review of *World's Fair*. In *America*
154 (8 March 1986), 193–194.
Calls the book a *bildungsroman* that illustrates
the universal quality of one Jewish boy's experiences.
Praises lyricism, but contends the novel is sometimes
overwritten.

235 Everhart, Nancy. Review of *Lives of the Poets: A
Novella and Six Short Stories*. In *Best Sellers* 44
(February 1985): 405.
States that the novella's prose captivates
readers and prompts identification with the narrator.
Sees short stories as being on various important
themes such as confrontation with death and mid-life
crises.

236 Falkenberg, Betty. "An Intruder Makes Good." *New
Leader: A Bi-Weekly of News and Opinion* 64 (12
January 1981), 16–17.
Describes *Loon Lake* as having an exhilarating
pace and a fine balance between risk-taking and con-
trol. Contends, however, that Doctorow often too
abruptly leaves settings he's elaborately conjured and
that the end of the novel doesn't work.

237 Ferguson, Malcolm M. Review of *Big as Life*. In
Library Journal 91 (15 April 1966): 2086.
One paragraph review compares this novel to
Orson Welles' radiocast of H.G. Wells's *The War of the
Worlds* and sees hints of *Dr. Strangelove* in Doctorow's
novel. Contends, however, that the book has nothing
to recommend it.

238 Fessler, Aaron L. Review of *The Book of Daniel*. In
Library Journal 96 (15 June 1971): 2102.
One paragraph review describes *The Book of
Daniel* as a magnificent achievement. Praises it as a
work of fiction that portrays the current feeling of
dissent in America.

239 Fiction. *Booklist* 68 (15 September 1971): 82.
One-paragraph review suggests *The Book of*

Daniel is compelling and that it vividly captures the period from the end of World War II to the Vietnam War.

240 Fiction. *Booklist* 72 (15 September 1975): 24.
     One paragraph review says *Ragtime's* intricate blend of heterogeneous characters creates nostalgia for a more-certain past.

241 Fleming, Thomas J. "Nude Giants in Fun City." *New Leader: A Bi-Weekly of News and Opinion* 49 (24 October 1966), 25-26.
     Sees *Big as Life* as a popular science fiction novel whose plot cannot be taken seriously.

242 Flower, Dean. "Fiction Chronicle." *The Hudson Review* 34 (Spring 1981), 105-116.
     Reviews *Loon Lake* and several other books. Believes Doctorow's novel is an ineffective pastiche of work by Mailer, Dos Passos, Fitzgerald and others. Argues that its experimental technique serves no purpose.

243 ------. "Fables of Identity." *The Hudson Review* 39 (Summer 1986), 309-321.
     Reviews *World's Fair* and several other books. Says Doctorow's book evokes a period rather than tells a story of an individual's boyhood. Concludes that the novel disappoints because it has no personal, only a historical, voice.

244 Fremont-Smith, Eliot. Making Book. *Village Voice,* 7 July 1975, 41.
     Suggests *Ragtime* is a fine novel, but its merit is not in using history imaginatively, which writers have always done. Rather, *Ragtime's* strength is in the subtext that explores a need to find patterns in and apply logic to seemingly random events.

245 ------. Making Book. *Village Voice,* 17 November 1975, 55.
     Comments on *Ragtime* as one of the year's best-selling hardcover books. Challenges Kramer's review (item 290) and maintains that *Ragtime* is an elegant tale, not an ideological tract.

246 ------. Making Book: Season's Greetings. *Village Voice,* 17 September 1980, 39.

Briefly comments on the difficulty of reviewing *Loon Lake* and suggests it will be viewed as wonderful, but flawed.

247 ------. "The Trickle Down Theory of Uplift." *Village Voice*, 31 December 1980, 32-33.
Reports on winners of National Book Critics Circle Awards and gives his own evaluation of each book. Calls *Loon Lake* an interesting failure that never delivers a promised epiphany or makes a serious statement on social justice.

\ 248 French, Phillip. "In Darkest Disneyland." *New Statesman: An Independent Political and Literary Review* 91 (23 January 1976), 103-104.
Says *Ragtime* is a deceptively simple novel that probes political divisions and social turbulence in America's ragtime era, and also treats inexplicable mystical connections in life. Contends Doctorow is comparable to Pynchon or Borges.

· 249 Fuller, Edmund. "The Good Old Days, Jazzed Up a Bit." *The Wall Street Journal*, 17 July 1975, 18.
Calls *Ragtime* an accomplished "black nostalgia" novel, sentimentalizing an era which Doctorow shows deserves no nostalgia.

250 Gloag, Julian. Review of *Big as Life*. In *Kirkus Reviews* 34 (1 February 1966): 146.
Summarizes the plot and says Doctorow writes well enough to make it believable.

251 Gold, Herbert. Review of *Lives of the Poets: A Novella and Six Short Stories*. In *Los Angeles Times Book Review*, 25 November 1984, 1.
Calls the collection moving, entertaining and experimental. Applauds the novella's treatment of the writer's life in our contemporary age.

252 Gray, Paul. "The Nightmare and the Dream." *Time* 116 (22 September 1980), 81.
Believes that in *Loon Lake* Doctorow may try to do too much, but its historical reconstruction is strong and its prose effectively suggests the clashes of the Depression Era.

· 253 Green, Martin. "Nostalgia Politics." *The American Scholar* 45 (Winter 1976): 841-845.

Sees *Ragtime* as a novel written in a new historical genre that faithfully depicts eras and takes gross liberties with their personages. Criticizes its combination of nostalgia and revolutionary politics because this prompts readers to side with revolutionaries. Despite this shortcoming the novel indicates Doctorow's talent.

‘254   Greenland, Colin. "Rag Time." *New Statesman: An Independent Political and Literary Review* 111 (14 February 1986), 27.
Reviews *World's Fair* and four other books. Describes Doctorow's novel as fiction with the feel and detail of a documentary.

‘255   Griffin, L.W. Review of *Ragtime*. *Library Journal* 104 (July 1975): 1344.
One paragraph review praises book for impressionistically applying facts in an imaginative reinvention of early twentieth century America.

256   Grumbach, Doris. "Fine Print." *New Republic* 173 (5 July 1975), 30-31.
Predicts *Ragtime* will be one of the year's most popular and critically acclaimed books. Praises the quality of its prose which reproduces ragtime rhythms, as well as the book's authentic dialogue and intricate plot.

257   Guereschi, Edward. Review of *Loon Lake*. In *Best Sellers* 40 (December 1980): 310-311.
Sees this novel as completing a trilogy including *The Book of Daniel* and *Ragtime*, and finds underpinnings of the Grail Legend in *Loon Lake*. Believes the book is fascinating, even if its stylistic innovations sometimes obscure meaning.

258   Hackett, Alice P. *Forecasts*. *Publishers Weekly* 199 (12 April 1971): 75.
Says *The Book of Daniel* is a gripping and provocative saga of the agony of the children of the Atom Spies and a novel which successfully recreates different periods and places.

259   Halio, Jay L. "Contemplation, Fiction and the Writer's Sensibility." *Southern Review: Literary and Interdisciplinary Essays* 19 (Winter 1983): 203-218.
Reviews *Loon Lake* with several other novels.

Contends that open-ended novels are effective if the writer has technical virtuosity. However, *Loon Lake* is extremely pretentious. Furthermore, its characters reflect the seamy side of Depression life, but are not touching.

260 Harris, Mark. Review of *Loon Lake*. In *New Republic* 183 (20 September 1980), 31-34.
Argues the novel is a failure. Says the story is one Doctorow has already told, the stylistic innovations are pointless, and its characters are undeveloped. Also criticizes the book's promotion by Random House.

▼261 Hart, Jeffrey. "Doctorow Time." *National Review: A Journal of Fact and Opinion* 27 (15 August 1975), 892-893.
Praises *Ragtime*'s narrative thrust and its depiction of the ragtime era, but criticizes left-wing sentimentality glorifying revolutionaries and immigrants.

262 Hattman, John W. Review of *Big as Life*. *Best Sellers* 26 (1 June 1966): 86-87.
Says the novel is optimistic about people's ability to persevere in crises, but ultimately is marred by overly graphic sex scenes and negative view of organized religion.

263 Hendrickson, Paul. "Fact, Fiction, *Ragtime*: Fascinatin' Rhythms of a Lively Age." *National Observer* 2 August 1975, 19.
Contends the novel captures the feel of American life at the early part of the twentieth century. Relates ragtime music to the book's blend of historical and familial plots.

264 Hill, William B. Book Reviews: Fiction. *America* 133 (15 November 1975), 331-333.
Reviews *Ragtime* with several other novels. Describes marvelous sketches book gives of the ragtime era.

265 Hoberman, J. "Back to the Future." *Village Voice*, 26 November 1985, 57.
Suggests Doctorow fits Fiedler's definition of the practitioner of "mythological Americanism," and *World's Fair* is an American Jewish *bildungsroman* grappling with issues of Jewish identity, ambition and

politics in addition to the usual *bildungsroman* issues. Yet the novel is weak because it is too sentimental, not sufficiently visionary.

266   Hochschild, Adam.   "Radical Novelist."   *Progressive* 39 (September 1975), 56–57.
       Reviews *The Book of Daniel* and *Ragtime*.   Calls *The Book of Daniel* an eloquent radical novel whose language gives it great force.   Believes *Ragtime* has a similar concern with the historical moment and is a successful prose experiment, but *The Book of Daniel* is a better novel.

267   Howard, Maureen.   "Recent Novels: A Backward Glance."   *The Yale Review: A National Quarterly* 65 (March 1976): 404–413.
       Reviews *Ragtime* and nine other books.   Looks at recent fiction probing personal and national origins.   In this context, argues *Ragtime*'s assumptions of liberal comradery are too thin for fiction; novel ultimately partronizes readers and lacks a sense of history and social problems.   Reviewer states that novelists should avoid both sentimentality and documentation found in many current works.   The serious treatment of past by some writers is encouraging.

268   Howes, Victor.   "Spinning a Magic Cinematic Tale." *The Christian Science Monitor* 67 (14 August 1975), 22.
       Calls *Ragtime* a fascinating tale dominated by a motif of metamorphosis and says Doctorow has Walter Scott's historical imagination and Hemingway's ear.

269   Hrico, Bernard (Rev.).   Review of *The Book of Daniel*. *Best Sellers* 31 (15 August 1971): 218–219.
       Describes the novel as the accomplishment of a writer who knows what he wants to say, but suggests effects are contrived for polemical ends.

270   Iannone, Carol.   "E.L. Doctorow's 'Jewish' Radicalism." *Commentary* 81 (March 1986), 53–56.
       Argues Doctorow's work is not influenced by Judaism; rather it is influenced by his left-wing ideals.   Discusses how ideological bias undermines each work from *Welcome to Hard Times* to *World's Fair*.

271   Iyer, Pico.   "Going Through the Emotions."   *Partisan Review*   53 (Winter 1986): 132–137.

Reviews *Lives of the Poets: A Novella and Six Short Stories* with *Young Hearts Crying* by Richard Yates. Finds Doctorow's short stories arresting, but feels they have little resonance and are at times poorly written. Believes the novella fails to tie the stories together, and is a superficial, self-pitying tale embarrassingly close to Doctorow's life.

272 Johnson, Diane. "Waiting for Righty." *New York Review of Books* 27 (6 November 1980, 18-20.
Calls *Loon Lake* formally ambitious and debonair, but believes readers' responses to the novel will depend upon their class background. Fears Doctorow's continued need to assert his political position may flatten his characters, but concludes Doctorow is one of the bravest and most interesting contemporary American novelists.

273 Jones, D.A.N. "Bags." *Listener* 87 (17 February 1972), 221.
Reviews *The Book of Daniel* and four other books. Implicitly criticizes Doctorow's novel for its gory details and unsuccessful use of various tones and dialects.

274 ------. "Sour Truths." *Listener* 115 (8 May 1986), 26.
Reviews *World's Fair* and two other books. Describes Doctorow's novel as being deceptively simple, rich in period detail, and perhaps suggesting the emergence of Jewish-American writers.

*275 Kapp, Isa. "*Ragtime* Razzle-Dazzle." *New Leader: A Bi-Weekly of News and Opinion* 58 (15 September 1975), 15-17.
Evaluates this novel as one that concentrates on social forces rather than psychological dynamics, and thus leaves readers hungry for characters. Concludes *Ragtime* has little more than a movie-like, panoramic scope.

276 ------. "Tales of the Bronx." *New Leader: A Bi-Weekly of News and Opinion* 68 (16-30 December 1985), 5-6.
Briefly comments on *The Book of Daniel*, *Ragtime* and *Loon Lake*. Believes *World's Fair*'s trueness to childhood experience makes it Doctorow's best novel because the material sensitizes him to psychological

nuances. The book is marrred, however, by gratuitous details and inflated rhetoric.

277   Kauffmann, Stanley. "Wrestling Society for a Soul." *New Republic* 164 (5 June 1971), 25-27.
        Argues that *The Book of Daniel* is the best American political novel since Lionel Trilling's *The Middle of the Journey*. Praises Doctorow's novel for its examination of the Rosenbergs' legacy, its effective stylistic innovations and its character development.

278   ------. "A Central Vision." *Saturday Review: A Review of Literature and the Creative Arts* 2 (26 July 1975), 20-22.
        Says *Ragtime* is written exquisitely in ragtime rhythm meant to capture the changing nature of American life. Calls the novel an epic whose strength is in imaginatively dramatizing history.

279   Kazin, Alfred. "Alfred Kazin on Fiction." *New Republic* 173 (6 December 1975), 18-19.
        Reviews *Ragtime* with several other books. Says American novelists have mastered stylistic tricks, but often fill experimental novels with prefabricated characters. Explicitly says little of *Ragtime* other than calling it a made-to-order best-seller.

280   ------. "Left-Wing Melodrama: E.L. Doctorow's Novel About the Thirties." *Esquire* 94 (October 1980), 111.
        Finds *Loon Lake* disappointing, and speculates this is because Doctorow's intelligence is not equal to his creative talent. Believes Doctorow has a sentimental, simple view of labor. Argues that *Loon Lake*'s images are beautiful, but they are not infused with intellectual significance.

281   Keates, Jonathan. "The Day of the Wimp." *Observer* (9 February 1986), 26.
        World's Fair is reviewed with three other books. Reviewer says Doctorow is faithful to childhood experience, but his approach is too earnest and the world he evokes seems one-dimensional.

282   Kemp, Peter. "Of Men and Moles." *Listener* 104 (4 December 1980), 765.
        Discusses *Loon Lake* and four other books. Says that beneath surface innovations, the story of *Loon Lake* is simplistic and the dialogue is weak. The

novel captures the feel of the 1930s, but says nothing substantive about the period.

283 Kermode, John Frank. "Those Were the Days." *New Review* 2 (1976): 57-59.

Believes *Ragtime*'s theme that injustice endures through generations has no bite: the book is a superficial one with engaging, polished prose. Kermode makes his point by comparing *Ragtime* with other historical novels, particularly George Eliot's *Middlemarch* and Lionel Trilling's *The Middle of the Journey*; and by comparing it with Doctorow's other historical novels, which Kermode believes have more philosophical resonance.

284 King, Richard H. "Two Lights That Failed." *Virginia Quarterly Review: A National Journal of Literature and Discussion* 57 (Spring 1981): 341-350.

Loon Lake is reviewed with *The Second Coming* by Walker Percy. Review analyzes the reasons for each work's failure. Believes the social-political questions implied by *Loon Lake* require more probing. The novel is formally impressive, but fails to engage readers' minds or emotions to a sufficient degree.

285 Kitching, Jessie. Forecasts. *Publishers Weekly* 189 (7 February 1966): 88.

Sees *Big as Life* as a valiant attempt to come to grips with the idea of apocalypse, but contends the effort is thwarted because the novel's characters are not sufficiently developed and the author cannot imagine the endangered city's plight.

286 Klausler, Alfred P. "Portrait of an Era." *Christian Century: An Ecumenical Weekly* 2 (3 September 1975), 771.

Recommends *Ragtime* as a complex book that gives a provocative picture of the ragtime era.

287 Koenig, Rhoda. Review of *World's Fair*. In *New York* 18 (25 November 1985), 96-97.

Finds book plotless and dull. Furthermore, resents the fact that it treats the American Jewish experience in the 1930s as if it were the first fictional work to deal with this subject.

288 Koger, Grove. Review of *Lives of the Poets: A Novella and Six Short Stories*. In *Library Journal* 109 (15

November 1984): 2161.
Says the collection has merit, although it lacks
the panache of *Ragtime*.

289 Kornblum, Lee F. Review of *Drinks Before Dinner*. In
Library Journal 104 (15 June 1979): 1353.
One paragraph review. Concludes the drama is
a "play of ideas" with static characters and is thus
dull. Suspects, however, that the play's rhetoric
makes it more interesting to read than to view.

290 Kramer, Hilton. "Political Romance." *Commentary* 60
(October 1975), 76-80.
Classifies *Ragtime* as a romance rather than a
novel. Sees this book as a reflection of the anti-
American politics that surfaced in the 1960s, and contends reviewers' failure to note *Ragtime*'s leftist bias
is symptomatic of how deeply the myth of American
malevolence has penetrated the national psyche.
Criticizes the novel for distorting historical material
for ideological ends.
For rebuttal see item 245.

291 ------. "Yesterday's World of Tomorrow." *The Wall
Street Journal*, 7 February 1986, 19.
Sees *World's Fair* as a typical "first novel" in
which childhood recollections are reproduced without
regard for their narrative interest. Finds sensibility
of romanticizing childhood befits Doctorow, who has
always written conventionalized historical romances.

292 Kriegel, Leonard. "The Stuff of Fictional History."
Commonweal 102 (19 December 1975): 631-632.
Praises *Ragtime* for innovatively recreating history through a novel, but laments its sketchy characterizations. Posits this novel may point to a new
direction for the American novel which is usually
bound by individuality.

293 Kroll, Steven. "The Private Truth." *Book World* 5 (1
August 1971), 21.
Summarizes *The Book of Daniel*'s plot and
describes the book as a brutal personal and national
history in which Daniel, like his biblical predecessor,
endures at a terrible cost.

294 La Hood, Marvin J. Review of *World's Fair*. In *World
Literature Today: A Literary Quarterly of the*

University of Oklahoma 61 (Winter 1987): 101.
Says *World's Fair* is an exceptionally evocative
novel about growing up in the 1930s, although
novelistic hallmarks, such as plot and characterization,
are missing. *World's Fair* often seems like a documentary.

295 Lavoie, Thomas. Review of *Loon Lake*. In *Library
Journal* 105 (1 October 1980): 2105.
Describes this novel as Doctorow's most
challenging and complex one. Is impressed by the
book's symbolism and mythical implications.

296 ------. Review of *E.L. Doctorow: Essays and Conversations*. Library Journal 108 (1 May 1983): 907.
Describes the book as an interesting, if eclectic,
collection of primary and secondary articles and interviews. Finds the interviews are particularly useful
for articulating Doctorow's major concerns.
See item 58.

297 Leavitt, David. "Looking Back on the World of Tomorrow." *New York Review of Books* 90 (10 November
1985), 3, 25.
Sees *World's Fair* as attempting to blur the distinction between memory and imagination, between oral
history and fiction. The book is strong in depicting
the World's Fair as an imaginative escape, and suggesting that the faith and imagination of the main
character and the narrator offer hope. The amalgam
of genres, however, is uneven and thus does not
work.

298 Lee, Hermione. "Adultery in a Cold Climate." *Observer* 2 (November 1980), 29.
Reviews *Loon Lake* and three other books. Says
Doctorow's novel takes on important questions, but its
commentary on them is too obvious and its characters
are stereotypes.

299 Lehmann-Haupt, Christopher. "No Handwriting on the
Wall." *The New York Times*, 7 June 1971, 31.
Contends that *The Book of Daniel* is a major
novel that reflects the complexities of the Rosenberg
case and provides no easy answers.

300 ------. "A Newsreel About Our Family." *The New
York Times*, 8 July 1975, 29.

Contends *Ragtime* is successful because it reflects America's most significant conflicts in the last one hundred years. In an overview of Doctorow's work, reviewer says the author leapt to the ranks of first-rate novelists with *The Book of Daniel* and in *Ragtime* his imagination continues to produce work that is both experimental and accessible.

301   ------. Books of the Times. *The New York Times*, 6 November 1984, 15.
     Says the stories in *Lives of the Poets: A Novella and Six Short Stories* are best understood as part of the collection rather than individually. Believes the novella captures the autobiography of a writer's imagination and is on the whole more complex and richer than its ending.

302   ------. Books of the Times. *The New York Times*, 31 October 1985, 23.
     Praises *World's Fair* for being about the idea of the future in the mind of a developing child. Notes the persistence of movement toward the future in an epoch in which annihilation loomed.

303   Le Vot, André. Review of *Ragtime*. In *Espirit* (December 1976): 897-898.
     Praises silhouette effect and imitation of ragtime music in the novel. (in French)

304   Levy, Paul. "Historical Truth vs. Fiction." *Books and Bookmen* 21 (June 1976): 21-24.
     Argues that *Ragtime*'s plot is contrived to produce a best-seller. Some famous personages contribute nothing to the plot; the prose is bad, and the publisher's aggressive marketing is tasteless.

305   Lewis, Peter. "Two Noble Kinsmen, Et Cetera." *Stand Magazine* 27 (Summer 1986), 57-63.
     Reviews *World's Fair* and several other books. Deals with the theme of novels making social statements, and praises Doctorow's book as a highly successful *bildungsroman*. Finds the prose occasionally excessive.

306   Literature. *Booklist* 75 (15 July 1979): 1603.
     One paragraph review concludes *Drinks Before Dinner* is a rhetorical game lacking in dramatic skill.

307   Lodge, Sally A. Paperbacks, Fiction Reprints. *Publishers Weekly* 220 (6 October 1981): 76.
        Echoes the publication's earlier review that *Loon Lake* is an engaging novel, a "splendid achievement." See item 195.

308   Lottman, Eileen. Paperbacks, Fiction Reprints. *Publishers Weekly* 202 (24 July 1972): 76.
        Refers to some outstanding reviews the hardcover edition of *The Book of Daniel* received and describes the novel's plot as gripping.

309   Lucas, John. "Dust Behind the Dream." *Times Literary Supplement,* 7 November 1980, 1250.
        Sees *Loon Lake* as an intensely ambitious novel whose themes echo those of *The Great Gatsby.* Believes Doctorow's book is, however, contrived, and readers cannot actually feel for its characters.

310   Lyons, Bonnie. Review of *Lives of the Poets: A Novella and Six Short Stories.* In *Studies in Short Fiction* 22 (Spring 1985): 353-354.
        Finds best stories can stand independently, but the true power of the collection is its presentation of stories as the work of the novella's narrator and the complete work's critique of contemporary American life. Concludes that this experimental book combines social criticism with innovative writing in a way that is, ironically, mainstream Doctorow.

311   Maddocks, Melvin. Reviewer's Choice. *Life* 70 (25 June 1971), 14.
        Argues that *The Book of Daniel* is apolitical, advocating cultural rather than political revolution.

312   Maloff, Saul. "Critic's Choices for Christmas." *Commonweal* 95 (3 December 1971), 232.
        One-paragraph review praises *The Book of Daniel* for dealing with volatile emotions and sensitive political material without ever compromising itself.

313   ------. "Critic's Choices for Christmas." *Commonweal* 102 (5 December 1975), 600.
        One paragraph is devoted to *Ragtime.* Recommends novel as a satisfying blend of fact and fiction.

314   ------. "The American Dream in Fragments." *Commonweal* 107 (7 November 1980), 627-630.

Strongly praises *Loon Lake* for being able to use successfully a number of innovations, but believes Doctorow does not sufficiently develop some points in this story.

315 Mano, D. Keith. "That Trivial Finesse." *National Review: A Journal of Fact and Opinion* 38 (14 March 1986), 54-55.
Praises *World's Fair's* power to capture the past, but feels important events in the era and the main character's life are often lost in minor details.

316 Marcus, Greil. "*Loon Lake*: A Dip in Shallow Water." *Rolling Stone*, 30 October 1980, 31.
Contends the novel's crucial scenes don't resonate; images are often prefabricated or borrowed, and important episodes don't have enough detail to make them believable.

317 Mar-Jones, Adam. "Boosting the Status of the Text." *Times Literary Supplement*, 5 April 1985, 376A.
Finds the stories in *Lives of the Poet: A Novella and Six Short Stories* uneven and the novella too smug and full of small-minded details to be an effective exploration of a writer's life.

318 Marsh, Pamela. "On the Novel of Cruelty." *The Christian Science Monitor* 63 (17 June 1971), 11.
The Book of Daniel is one of two books reviewed. Reviewer focuses on the disturbing cruelty in *The Book of Daniel*, but concludes that Doctorow is talented and his book will endure.

319 "Martyrdom and After." *Times Literary Supplement*, 18 February 1972, 173.
Contends that in *The Book of Daniel* the technique of having Daniel write the account allows Doctorow to dodge blame for the subjects included, as well as the book's tone and exaggerated irony.

320 McLellan, Joseph. Paperbacks. *Book World* (25 July 1976): G4.
One paragraph review says *Ragtime* combines substance and readability.

321 McNamee, Martin. Review of *Drinks Before Dinner*. In *Best Sellers* 39 (October 1979): 262.
Concludes the play is primarily an experiment

in language that is likely to disappoint those expecting more conventional drama.

322 Moses, Joseph. "To Impose a Phrasing on History." *The Nation* 21 (4 October 1975): 310-312.
     States *Ragtime* imposes meaning on history through ambiguity, under and overstatement and rich use of metaphor. In a sense, the novel is about the artist's control over time.

323 Murray, James G. "Fiction in the (Very) Low 80s: An Early Retrospective with (Mostly) Regrets for the Future." *Critic* 39 (December 1980): 1-8.
     Review of several recent novels which focuses on documentary fiction. Sees *Loon Lake* as a stylistically brilliant novel echoing Transcendentalist concerns with time and experience.

324 Mutter, John. Paperbacks, Fiction Reprints. *Publishers Weekly* 228 (29 November 1985): 45.
     Recounts earlier praise for *Lives of the Poets: A Novella and Six Short Stories* (see item 373). Calls Doctorow an "impeccable stylist" who "finds fresh, touching metaphors for the human condition."

325 Nordell, Roderick. "Novelist as Small Boy: Doctorow Goes to the Fair." *The Christian Science Monitor* 78 (6 December 1985), B1.
     Praises *World's Fair* as an accurate account of growing up in the 1930s and a compelling memoir in the Wordsworthian vein.

326 "Notable Nominations." *American Libraries* 2 (October 1971): 1010.
     Reports that *The Book of Daniel* is under consideration as a Notable Book of 1971. Says this work is a moving novel that recreates the atmosphere of the McCarthy Era.

327 O'Connell, Shaun. "American Fiction, 1975: Celebration in Wonderland." *Massachusetts Review: A Quarterly of Literature, the Arts and Public Affairs* 17 (Spring 1976): 165-193.
     Devotes about three pages to *Ragtime*, stating that while the novel is often entertaining, its view of history is flat, its prose dull, and on the whole it is often too self-conscious.

328 Parrinder, Patrick. "Cover Stories." *London Review of Books* 7 (4 April 1985), 15–16.
    Reviews *Lives of the Poets: A Novella and Six Short Stories* with two other books. Points out that the women in Doctorow's collection are often portrayed as menacing or destructive. While two or three stories in this collection are memorable, the others are mediocre and the novella is little more than a chronicle of New York life.

329 Peden, William. "Recent Fiction: Some of the Best." *Western Humanities Review* 39 (Autumn 1985): 267–273.
    Calls *Lives of the Poets: A Novella and Six Short Stories* remarkable, the best piece of fiction published during the year. Admires the mix of genres in the stories and the novella, and the variety of narrative techniques.

330 Peters, Margaret. "Short Takes From the Author of *Ragtime*." *The Wall Street Journal*, 4 January 1985, 130.
    Finds individual stories in *Lives of the Poets: A Novella and Six Short Stories* to be powerful renditions of people haunted by personal history, but feels the novella is not the unifying force it was intended to be.

331 Petersen, Clarence. Review of *World's Fair*. In *Chicago Tribune*, 14 December 1986, 9.
    One paragraph review praises the fact that the novel's simple prose seems to be the work of a boy who chronicled the events shortly after they occurred.

332 Prescott, Peter S. "Lion's Den." *Newsweek* 77 (7 June 1971), 113–114.
    Calls *The Book of Daniel* a compelling and purgative novel about the heirs of the 1950s. Believes much of the novel's power is achieved through irony.

333 ------. "The Year in Books: A Personal Report." *Newsweek* 78 (27 December 1971), 57, 60–61.
    One paragraph review summarizes the plot of *The Book of Daniel* and describes the novel as angry and deeply felt.

334 ------. "Doctorow's Daring Epic." *Newsweek* 96 (15 September 1980), 88–89A.

States that despite innovations Doctorow is a traditional writer because *Loon Lake,* like his other works, deals with American history and myths. Finds the shifts in narration irritating and the quality of the prose uneven, but the story compelling.

335 ------. "The Creative Muse." *Newsweek* 104 (19 November 1984), 107, 108B.

Sees *Lives of the Poets: A Novella and Six Short Stories* as an outstanding work of fiction. The novella depicts a writer's struggle with midlife crisis; the stories in different ways portray deeply wounded people.

336 Raban, Jonathan. "Easy Virtue: On Doctorow's *Ragtime.*" *Encounter* 46 (February 1976), 71–74.

Posits novelists are attracted to journalistic writing because it is detached. Believes *Ragtime* fails precisely because it is too detached: There is little beneath the surface story of its characters' lives.

337 Ramsey, Nancy. Review of *Loon Lake.* In *New York Arts Journal* 22 (1981), 21–22.

Calls this novel a shallow, calculated work. Believes Doctorow indiscriminately borrows techniques from Dos Passos, Stein and Joyce. Finds *Loon Lake's* fast pace inappropriate for depicting the Great Depression, and says neither the plot nor characters are believable.

338 Review of *American Anthem.* In *Popular Photography* 90 (July 1983), 102.

Brief review finds Doctorow's "effectively antiphonal" prose complements pictures.

339 Review of *American Anthem.* In *Publishers Weekly* 222 (16 July 1982), 70.

Says Doctorow's prose often descends into bathos.

340 Review of *Big as Life.* In *Choice* 3 (November 1966), 769.

One paragraph review concludes the novel is a minor work and recommends it only for libraries with large holdings in the modern novel.

341 Review of *The Book of Daniel.* In *Kirkus Reviews* 39 (1 April 1971): 392.

Says readers of *The Book of Daniel* may question some of the Rosenberg story even in fictional form, but the novel is nonetheless riveting.

342 Review of *Drinks Before Dinner*. In *Choice* 16 (November 1979), 1170.
One paragraph review finds *Drinks Before Dinner* completely dull because, in its attempt to deal with the "language of ideas," it ignores visual imagery and other elements necessary for successful theater.

343 Review of *Lives of the Poets: A Novella and Six Short Stories*. In *Kirkus Reviews* 52 (15 September 1984): 868.
Finds this a slight collection without a distinctive voice, but says it offers some cerebral and political rewards for Doctorow's admirers.

344 Review of *Lives of the Poets: A Novella and Six Short Stories*. In *West Coast Review of Books* 11 (January 1985): 30.
Briefly summarizes the plot of the novella and the short stories.

345 Review of *Loon Lake*. In *Kirkus Reviews* 48 (15 July 1980): 923-924.
Finds this novel self-consciously avant garde and self-indulgent.

▶346 Review of *Ragtime*. In *Kirkus Reviews* 43 (1 May 1975): 529-530.
Praises the novel's accomplishment in beautifully depicting the true social situation of the era.

▼347 Review of *Ragtime*. In *The New York Times Book Review*, 28 December 1975, 1, 3.
Novel is one of thirteen books chosen by the Book Review staff as the year's best. One paragraph summarizes the plot and says the novel, with its combination of nostalgia and literary imagination, invites readers to dream about history.

348 Review of *Ragtime*. In *Psychology Today* 9 (October 1975), 100.
One paragraph review says book is rare in that it appeals to both critics and general readers. The novel is innovative and foreshadows significant social movements of the 1960s and 1970s.

349 Review of *World's Fair*. In *Booklist* 82 (15 September 1985): 90.
     One-paragraph review describes the novel as a gratifying piece of historical fiction.

350 Review of *World's Fair*. In *Book World* 16 (30 November 1986), 12.
     One paragraph review praises the boy's story for being universal enough to appeal to most readers.

351 Review of *World's Fair*. In *Kirkus Reviews* 53 (15 September 1985): 962.
     Praises *World's Fair* as Doctorow's best novel since *The Book of Daniel*. Believes *World's Fair's* strength is its careful rendition of a child growing up in a bygone era.

352 Review of *World's Fair*. In *Library Journal* 111 (January 1986): 46.
     Says the novel depicts family life in painstaking detail.

353 Review of *World's Fair*. In *Virginia Quarterly Review: A National Journal of Literature and Discussion* 62 (Spring 1986): 56.
     One paragraph review says the inclusion of other family members' memories makes the novel more complex, and readers who grew up in urban areas during the Depression will be especially moved by the story.

354 Review of *World's Fair*. In *West Coast Review of Books* 11 (November 1985), 25.
     Says the novel has delightful descriptions and a nostalgic feel, but it does not provide any understanding of the child's social context, thus *World's Fair* seems thin and fragmented.

355 Richmond, Jane. "To the End of the Night." *Partisan Review* 39 (1972): 627-629.
     Reviews *The Book of Daniel* and two other novels. Calls Doctorow's book a brilliant achievement, one of the best contemporary novels. Praises this novel for its handling of controversial historical figures, its treatment of crises and its attention to varieties of radical thought.

356 Runnells, Douglas C. "Restless Roads." *Christian Century: An Ecumenical Weekly* 98 (7 January 1981), 20-21.

      Sees *Loon Lake* as an interesting, satisfying attempt to render nonlinear thinking in narrative: Essentially, *Loon Lake* is a novel about narrative technique.

357 Sale, Roger. "From Ragtime to Riches." *New York Review of Books* 22 (7 August 1975), 21-22.

      Applauds contemporary tendency to mingle fact and fiction. Contends that the first half of *Ragtime* is more successful than the second, for after the Coalhouse Walker subplot begins, the actions of minor characters become more predictable. On the whole, the book is not entirely successful, but its vision and technique suggest possibilities for Doctorow and for fiction in general.

358 ------. "The Realms of Gold." *The Hudson Review* 28 (Winter 1975): 616-628.

      Ragtime is one of several books reviewed. Doctorow's novel is praised for its air of authenticity and its new, effective use of ragtime rhythm in fiction.

359 Schickel, Richard. Review of *The Book of Daniel*. In *Harper's Magazine* 243 (August 1971), 93-94.

      Praises this novel for its sensitive portrayal of the Isaacson children, its accurate rendition of a Stalinist mind and its capture of some semblance of truth. Has reservations about novel's parallels between the Old and New Left.

360 Schmitz, Neil. "Three Novels." *Partisan Review* 48 (1981): 629-633.

      Says *Loon Lake* is about reflection and about the writer's power to appropriate experience and thereby create new life.

361 Seelye, John. "Doctorow's Dissertation." *New Republic* 174 (10 April 1976), 21-23.

      Defends *Ragtime* against American reviewers' second thoughts and against harsh British reviews. Suggests *Ragtime* is a classic historical romance that effectively draws upon Dos Passos's work and Kleist's "Michael Kohlhaas."

362   Shelton, Frank W. Review of *World's Fair*. In *National Forum* (Summer 1986): 47.
        Describes the book as being about the process of memory and the nature of the American Dream. In this work the Dream is less pernicious than in Doctorow's other novels. Believes *World's Fair* is one of Doctorow's best works.

ᐟ363   Sheppard, R.Z. "The Music of Time." *Time* 106 (14 July 1975), 64, 66.
        Calls *Ragtime* a "fabulous tale" whose lyric tone and ragtime rhythm transcend interpretation. Includes brief biography.

364   ------. "The Artist as a Very Young Critic." *Time* 126 (18 November 1985), 100.
        Sees *World's Fair* as being too guarded with its material, more like a memoir than a novel because it does not utilize symbolism. Finds the child Edgar too verbose to be recognizable as a child or a budding novelist; the character seems more like a budding critic.

365   Shrimpton, Nicholas. "New Jersey Joe." *New Statesman: An Independent Political and Literary Review* 100 (31 October 1980), 27.
        Finds Doctorow's combined aesthetic and political concerns unique among contemporary writers, and believes Doctorow has trouble combining the two. *Loon Lake*'s thrust is limited, and in general Doctorow's work requires more subtlety of thought.

366   Sigal, Clancy. "A Better Yesterday." *Manchester Guardian Weekly* 23 February 1986, 21.
        Believes *World's Fair* is strong in capturing the details of a Bronx boyhood and presenting visual images. However, its story is too nostalgic and devoid of a child's growing pains and fears.

367   Skow, John. "Between Books." *Time* 124 (24 December 1984), 69-70.
        Says most of the short stories in *Lives of the Poets: A Novella and Six Short Stories* are forgettable, and suggests Doctorow is pausing between substantial works of fiction. Believes the novella is without a clear point, but it works because it is about a writer's difficulty in capturing life.

368 Sokolov, Raymond. Review of *Ragtime.* In *Book World* (13 July 1975): 1, 3.

   Praises the book for mixing historical facts with inventions or anachronisms, thus forcing readers to suspend disbelief. Says the novel appears simple and traditional, but it is actually stylistically innovative and does not follow traditional plot lines.

369 ------. "Doctorow's Oddly Appealing Fable of Wealth." *The Wall Street Journal,* 29 September 1980, 30.

   Finds *Loon Lake*'s self-conscious modernism and narrative shifts irritating, but thinks the story itself is compelling.

370 Stade, George. Review of *Ragtime.* In *The New York Times Book Review,* 6 July 1975, 1-2.

   Says the novel is Doctorow's most successful because, like the best experimental modern writing, its innovations serve the book's purpose: They recreate the feel of the era and absorb readers rather than simply embellish details.

371 ------. "Types Defamiliarized." *Nation* 231 (27 September 1980), 285-286.

   Argues that all of Doctorow's fiction defamiliarizes literary types and *Loon Lake* is a particularly ironic twist on the Horatio Alger stories. Comments on the significance of the name Korzeniowski and the theme of father-son rivalry in American literature. Believes the prose in *Loon Lake* is not as elegant as that in *Ragtime,* and Doctorow's social conscience sometimes makes the *Loon Lake* predictable. Nonetheless, this novel is ultimately more resonant than Doctorow's others.

372 Starr, Kevin. Review of *Welcome to Hard Times.* *New Republic* 173 (6 September 1975), 25-27.

   Written on novel's reissue. Discusses the Western as the genre of the outsider and as a lowbrow one capable of being transformed into high art. Doctorow takes a thin Western plot and turns it into an allegory of good and evil. In his first, strong novel Doctorow exhibits his feel for American myths.

373 Steinberg, Sybil. PW Forecasts. *Publishers Weekly* 226 (28 September 1984): 99.

   Praises impeccable style of all the works in *Lives of the Poets: A Novella and Six Short Stories* and says they deal effectively with theme of individual isolation. Contends that the novella and the short stories "Willi" and "The Writer in the Family" are classics. Summarized in item 324.

374 ------. PW Forecasts. *Publishers Weekly* 228 (13 September 1985): 124.
    Feature review of *World's Fair* claims this is Doctorow's most powerful novel. Says the book renders memories appropriate to the chronological age of the main character; it captures the era and the special circumstances of a Jewish boy growing up in it. The reviewer also praises the novel's lyrical quality.

375 Storms, C.G. Review of *Lives of the Poets: A Novella and Six Short Stories.* In *Choice* 22 (March 1985): 987.
    One paragraph review praises Doctorow's bold experiment depicting a writer's transformation of experience into art, but the reviewer believes this book is less compelling than *Ragtime* and *Loon Lake.*

376 Sutherland, John. "Edgar and Emma." *London Review of Books* 8 (20 February 1986), 18-19.
    Reviews *World's Fair* with a novel by Emma Tennant. Believes this to be Doctorow's best novel. Its fusion of fiction and autobiography permits a range of literary effects; its clipped, understated prose is highly effective.

377 Sylvander, Carolyn Wedin. Review of Levine, Paul, *E.L. Doctorow.* In *Moderna Sprak* 79 (4: 1985): 357-358
    Finds Levine's book most helpful in clarifying *Welcome to Hard Times, The Book of Daniel* and *Ragtime.* Believes its treatment of *Loon Lake* is less convincing and expresses regret that, as Levine points out, *Loon Lake* signals an autobiographical turn for Doctorow.
See item 55.

378 Tennant, Emma. "Boneyard." *Listener* 95 (22 January 1976), 92.
    Criticizes *Ragtime* for irresponsibly and dangerously mingling fact and fiction. Suggests this novel was written for the American mass market.

379 Theroux, Paul. "Versions of Exile." *Encounter* 38 (May 1972), 69-73.

Reviews *The Book of Daniel* with several other books. In one paragraph describes how Daniel's cruelty seems attributable to his hatred of America where he remains alienated and bitter.

380   Thwaite, Anthony. "Po-Faced Pretensions." *Observer*, 18 January 1976, 30.
Reviews *Ragtime* and two other books. Finds *Ragtime* too self-consciously clever and superficial. Suggests the novel's readability and the power of the Coalhouse Walker subplot may account for the book's popularity in America.

381   ------. "Dogged Provincialism." *Observer*, 31 March 1985, 26.
Finds stories and novella in *Lives of the Poets: A Novella and Six Short Stories* mediocre. Says Doctorow's American appeal doesn't carry over to Britain.

382   Todd, Richard. "The Most-Overrated-Book of the Year Award and Other Literary Prizes." *Atlantic Monthly* 237 (January 1976), 95-96.
Features *Ragtime* in a review with five other books. Contends that while *Ragtime* is entertaining, it is all style--empty of serious social analysis and political content.

383   Towers, Robert. "A Brilliant World of Mirrors." *The New York Times Book Review*, 28 September 1980, 1+.
Describes *Loon Lake* as exhilarating. Its play on doubleness and its human substance make it compelling, even if its diverse themes and images lack coherence.

384   ------. "Light and Lively." *New York Review of Books* 31 (6 December 1984), 33-34.
Lives of the Poets: A Novella and Six Short Stories is one of two books reviewed. Reviewer finds little sense in reading short stories and novella as part of one collection or in autobiographically reading the novella. He believes this book is not comparable to Doctorow's best novels, but it does give an interesting portrait of the artist during a mid-life crisis.

385   ------. "Three Part Inventions." *New York Review of Books* 32 (19 December 1985), 23.
World's Fair is reviewed with two other novels.

Reviewer discusses the book's blurring of autobiography and fiction, its mingling of childhood and adult perceptions and its rich detail of 1930s. He concludes that the novel is an excellent autobiography, but it lacks the suspense of good fiction.

386 Treadwell, T.O. "Time-Encapsulating." *Times Literary Supplement*, 14 February 1986, 163.

Concludes that *World's Fair*, by focusing on the experience of one boy growing up in the Depression, more effectively renders its era than *Ragtime* or *Loon Lake* did theirs. Compares *World's Fair* to James Joyce's *A Portrait of the Artist as a Young Man*.

387 Tyler, Anne. "A Child's Garden of Memories Pervades *World's Fair*." *The Detroit News*, 10 November 1985, B6.

Praises the novel as a time capsule of an era. Believes the book is particularly strong because it captures a child's keen observations.

388 Tytell, John. Review of *Loon Lake*. In *American Book Review* 3 (November/December 1980): 6.

Concludes this novel is less powerful than *Ragtime* and *The Book of Daniel* because of its gratuitous details, and its scant characterizations. It lacks the fable qualities that shaped *Ragtime*.

389 Upfront: Advance Reviews, Adult Fiction. *Booklist* 81 (1 October 1984): 146.

Summary review in one paragraph ends recommending the collection *Lives of the Poets: A Novella and Six Short Stories* as best when read cover to cover.

390 Upfront: Advance Reviews, Adult Fiction. *Booklist* 77 (1 September 1980): 4.

One-paragraph review of *Loon Lake* finds this novel disappointing. Faults narrative structure and ponderous mood.

391 Wade, Rosalind. Quarterly Fiction Review. *Contemporary Review* 228 (April 1976): 213-216.

Ragtime is one of six novels reviewed. The reviewer concludes that the novel's characters are difficult to identify with and the United Kingdom's readers are unlikely to find the novel interesting.

392   Wall, Stephen. "Fathers and Failures." *Observer* 20
      February 1972, 28.
          Reviews *The Book of Daniel* and three other
      books. Finds the scenes focusing on family drama
      more probing than the sections of the book dealing
      with larger political questions.

393   Waugh, Auburn. "Prophet and Loss." *Spectator* 228
      (19 February 1972), 276-277.
          Argues that Doctorow began *The Book of Daniel*
      with an interesting idea--to investigate the fate of
      children whose parents had been executed for
      espionage. The novel's purpose, however, quickly be-
      comes the polemical one of condemning the
      Rosenbergs' executions and the investigations of the
      McCarthy era.

394   White, Edmund. "Pyrography." *Nation* 241 (30 Novem-
      ber 1985), 594-595.
          Praises *World's Fair* as an autobiographical
      novel that is confident with its material and illustrates
      that the typical American life is in many respects
      atypical. Finds the characters and the period clearly
      drawn.

395   Wiehe, Janet. Review of *World's Fair*. In *Library
      Journal* 110 (15 October 1985): 101.
          Describes the book as moving and says it
      recreates both the specific Depression era it depicts
      and the universal elements of the main character's
      childhood.

396   Wolcott, James. "Rag Time." *New Republic* 191 (3
      December 1984), 31-34.
          Finds *Lives of the Poets: A Novella and Six
      Short Stories* fragmented and pretentious. Believes
      that the novella's focus on the writer's physical and
      emotional malaise betrays petty vanity. Reviewer
      questions that the writer's mission is to tell the truth
      with verisimilitude, and suggests that in fiction the
      truth must be transformed.

397   Yardley, Jonathan. "Ruminations and Regrets." *Book
      World* 14 (11 November 1984): 3.
          Thinks the novella in the collection *Lives of the
      Poets: A Novella and Six Short Stories* captures the
      quality of New York City life and the preoccupations
      of its self-indulgent residents. Thus the novella is

good social commentary. However, it fails to il-
luminate the writer's crisis. The short stories are
well-written, with particularly strong sections, but
they are not obviously the work of the writer
depicted in the novella.

DRAMA REVIEWS

398 *Drinks Before Dinner.* Directed by Mike Nichols.
Public/Newman Theater. Opened 24 October 1978.
Closed 3 December 1978. Limited engagement of forty-
eight performances.

Reviews

399 Barnes, Clive. "'Dinner' Is Unfulfilling." *The New
York Times*, 24 November 1978, 39.
Praises the staging and acting, but finds the
dialogue and plot pretentious and empty.

400 Beaufort, John. "Novelist Doctorow Fashions a Play of
Ideas." *The Christian Science Monitor*, 30 November
1978, 19.
Believes this play fails to flesh out its characters, but simply presents them as types of the era.
Praises the Public Theater's presentation of a highly
intellectual work.

401 Clurman, Harold. Review in *Nation* 227 (16 December
1978), 685–686.
Reviews with one other play. Finds Doctorow's
play undramatic because it lacks action and its
dialogue is mundane. Admires its casting.

402 Eder, Richard. "Doctorow's *Drinks Before Dinner*."
The New York Times, 24 November 1978, C4.
Believes this work is more like a platonic
dialogue than a play, but finds it has some dramatic
moments and believes the theme of world destroying
itself is worth attention. Praises the acting.

403 Kalem, T.E. Review in *Time* 112 (4 December 1978),
108.
Suggests that the play's themes have previously

been stated more effectively by major writers and that on the whole this drama is dull and empty.

404   Kroll, Jack. "Cocktail Party." *Newsweek* 92 (4 December 1978), 131.

      Summarizes the plot and concludes that, although the play is somewhat self-indulgent, it is an effective representation of the contemporary dread of apocalypse.

405   Oliver, Edith. The Theatre. *The New Yorker* 54 (4 December 1978), 84–86.

      Reviews several plays. Finds *Drinks Before Dinner* thoroughly boring, full of banalities and pretentious monologues.

406   Sharp, Christopher. Review in *Women's Wear Daily*, 27 November 1978, 12.

      Says the play is an interior monologue, not a drama. Does not find the plot believable.

407   Simon, John. "Books Before Drama." *The New Yorker* 11 (11 December 1978), 117–118.

      Finds the play is tedious and has few theatrical qualities. Particularly criticizes the dialogue as artificial and awkward.

408   Watt, Douglass. "There's One at Every Party." *Daily News*, 24 November 1978, Section 2, 5.

      Tongue-in-cheek review finds play pretentious and dull.

Drinks Before Dinner

409   Radio Play Production. Directored by Yuri Rasovsky. National Radio Theatre of Chicago.

Review

410   Troop, Elizabeth. Plays in Performance. *Drama: The Quarterly Theatre Review.* 149 (1983): 38.

      Reviews several radio plays. Finds the language in Doctorow's play witty and a faithful rendition of New York speech, but says the play is boring because all the characters sound like the author.

FILMS AND FILM REVIEWS

Film

411   *Welcome to Hard Times* (British title: *Killer on a Horse*). Directed by Burt Kennedy. Produced by Max E. Youngstein and David Karr. Screenplay by Burt Kennedy. Metro-Goldwyn-Mayer, 1967.

Reviews

412   Britt, Gweneth. *Films in Review* 18 (May 1967): 310.
        States that the story line is implausible, the dialogue is confusing and inappropriate and Burt Kennedy's direction is inept. Sees this film as a complete disaster.

413   Crist, Judith. "An Adult Western--Almost." *New York World Journal Tribune*, 2 May 1967, 19.
        Believes this ambitious Western began well in faithful allegiance to Doctorow's novel, but ultimately floundered because the Bad Man became just another criminal, not the embodiment of evil he is in the book. Furthermore, Kennedy added a sentimental happy ending.
        Listed in item 420.

414   Crowther, Bosley. *The New York Times*, 2 May 1967, 56.
        Finds the characters unrealistic, and the film as a whole listless and haphazard.
        Listed in item 420.

415   Farber, Stephen. *Film Quarterly* 21 (Fall 1967): 49-58.
        Reviewed with *Hombre* as a Western film that subverts standard Western myths. Argues against the prevailing view that the film is a parable of good

against evil; instead sees its familial and sexual tension as symbolizing the struggle between impulse and civilization. Despite its interesting theme, the reviewer feels the film lacks conviction and does not sufficiently explore interpersonal dynamics.

416 Gill, Brendan. Current Cinema. *The New Yorker* 43 (13 May 1967), 178, 181.
        Reviews *Welcome to Hard Times* and several other films. Sees the film based on Doctorow's book as a dreary parable of good and evil masquerading as a Western. Finds the film dull because its scenes, characters and dialogue are all predictable.

417 Hanson, Curtis Lee. Point of View. *Cinema* 3 (Summer 1967): 50.
        Reviewed with three other films. Praises Kennedy's screenplay for capturing the attitudes of the West and calls the acting first-rate. Comments on the theme that surviving is more important than acting courageously.

418 Junker, Howard. "Bad Day at Hard Times." *Newsweek* 69 (8 May 1967), 104.
      Summarizes the plot and concludes the film is overly symbolic.

419 Review in *America* 116 (20 May 1967), 764.
        Sees film as a frustrating jumble of events filled with senseless brutality.

420 Review in *Filmfacts*. 10 (March 1967): 111.
        Gives synopsis of plot and summarizes reviews from *The New York Times*, *Variety*, *New York World Journal Tribune*, and *Time*.
      See items 413, 414, 421, 424.

421 Review in *Variety*. 29 March 1967, 26.
        Says acting, direction and script all fail; moreover, the beginning and end of the film are too brutal.
      Listed in item 420.

422 Schickel, Richard. "Neorealism in the Old Corral." *Life* 62 (26 May 1967), 14.
        Thinks the film is often boring, but nonetheless praises its director for attempting to make a thought-provoking Western movie.

423 Sheed, Wilfrid. In *Esquire* 68 (August 1967), 30, 34.
Reviewed with several other films. Finds
Fonda's performance as Blue too earnest and the film
on the whole dull.

424 "Tired Palomino." *Time* 89 (12 May 1967), 102.
Describes this film as a tired collection of old
Western types and themes that is only partially
redeemed by its outstanding acting.
Listed in item 420.

425 Winsten, Archer. *New York Post.* 2 May 1967, 64.
Believes the film fails because it tries too hard
for grand effects and theme, strains too much in
trying to be more than an ordinary Western.

Film

426 *Ragtime.* Directed by Miloš Forman. Produced by
Dino De Laurentiis. Screenplay by Michael Weller.
Paramount Pictures, 1981.

Reviews

427 Asahina, Robert. "Sorting Out the Film Glut." *New
Leader: A Bi-Weekly of News and Opinion* 65 (25
January 1982), 20-21.
Reviewed with several other films. Calls *Ragtime*
a disaster. Direction is overstylized; some parts of
the novel are overemphasized, while others are
thoughtlessly dropped.

428 Benayoun, Robert. "La Temps Por Lambeau ou Time in
Rags." *Positif* 250 (January 1982): 79-82.
Sees *Ragtime* as representative of Hollywood's
film evolution and finds merit in the idea of history's
volatility. (in French)

429 Benson, Sheila. Review in *Los Angeles Times,* 15
November 1981, Calendar 29.
States that while the novel proceeded at a fast
pace and had an optimistic tone, the film lacks these.
Furthermore, the film has few historical personages
and little sense of history. Individual performances
are praised.

430 Bonitzer, Pascal. "Un Epopee de la Dissidence."
Cahiers du Cinema 331 (January 1982): 44-46.
Contends that for all its diverse strains, this

film is essentially about American dissidents and their evolution in the 1960s. Praises Forman's art and casting. (in French)

431 Boyum, Joy Gould. "Didn't Anyone Read the Book?" *The Wall Street Journal*, 20 November 1980, 31.
   Believes that the novel's panoramic scope invites filming, but Forman's adaptation failed because it overemphasized Coalhouse's story and diminished the novel's politics and sense of history.

432 Buckley, Michael. Review in *Films in Review* 33 (January 1982): 48-49.
   Praises the acting, but believes the extensive subplot on Coalhouse Walker's ordeal lacks suspense. Finds the film interesting, but ultimately disappointing.

433 Buckley, Tom. "The Forman Formula." *The New York Times Magazine*, 1 March 1981, 28+.
   Focuses on Forman's decision to include only some key episodes in the film *Ragtime* and discusses some of his casting decisions. Gives Forman's biography.

434 Canby, Vincent. "Film *Ragtime* Evokes Real and Fictional Pasts." *The New York Times*, 20 November 1981, C10.
   Says that while the film is entertaining and its acting is good, *Ragtime* ultimately fails because it is a series of incoherent vignettes. Argues that the book's strong point was showing two types of people: those who profited by art of duplication and those who lost. The film cannot convey this point.

435 ------. "Acting Gems of '81." *The New York Times*, 10 January 1982, Section 2, 15.
   Briefly mentions Mandy Patinkin's performance as an outstanding one that might have pulled the film together if his role hadn't been minimized.

436 Coleman, John. Review in *New Statesman: An Independent Political and Literary Review* 103 (19 February 1982), 29-30.
   Reviewed with *Priests of Love*. Praises *Ragtime*'s panoramic quality and fine acting, but wishes the Coalhouse Walker episode didn't dominate and other parts of the novel, such as Ford's meeting with Morgan, had been included.

437 Combs, Richard. "One Man's Sense of Honour." *The
Times Literary Supplement*, 26 February 1982, 215.
Believes that in emphasizing Coalhouse's story
Forman creates a polemical message that is not in the
novel. Furthermore, without the social forces represented by Emma Goldman and J.P. Morgan, Coalhouse's
story lacks context.

438 ------. *Monthly Film Bulletin* 49 (March 1982): 46.
Believes this film adaptation is marred by lack
of narrative continuity that successfully wove
together the novel's diverse strains. The book's historical sense and mystical intuition are missing; its
historical personages are greatly reduced.

439 Corliss, Richard. "One More Sad Song." *Time* 118 (23
November 1981), 97.
Says Forman is an actor's director who elicits
fine performances and the film has moments of
emotional grandeur, but on the whole it lacks the
novel's energetic movement.

440 Coursodon, Jean-Pierre. "*Ragtime: La Question di
Choix.*" *Cinema* 278 (February 1982): 77-79.
Says a social conscience informed the novel
Ragtime and the film *Reds*, but this conscience is ab-
sent from the film *Ragtime*. The absence of major
figures that were in the novel is likewise regrettable.
Although the film falls far short of the book's ambi-
tions, it is not, as some have charged, a mere series
of vignettes. (in French)

441 Crist, Judith. "Dazzling *Ragtime*." *Saturday Review:
A Review of Literature and the Arts* 8 (December
1981), 66, 69.
States that the film captures the meaning and
rhythm of Doctorow's novel about a crucial age in
American history. Praises costumes, cinematography
and casting.

442 Denby, David. "Slow Motion." *New York* 14 (30 November 1981), 63-65.
Believes that while the novel was entertaining,
the movie is dull because some of the book's choice
scenes are omitted and the dominance of the Coalhouse
Walker subplot suggests an overly-serious liberal con-
scientiousness.

443 Desrues, Hubert. Review in *La Revue du Cinema* 368 (January 1982): 38-40.
Summarizes the film's plot and says, despite the difficulty of dealing with the theme of racism, the film's dialogue is effective and its staging is beautiful. (in French)

444 "Eight Holiday Films." *The Washington Post*, 18 December 1981, Weekend, 17.
Says the film fails to capture the sense of the ragtime era because the book's background information on the three families and its celebrities is missing. As the story of Coalhouse Walker's ordeal, however, the film is effective.

445 Eyles, Allen. Review in *Films & Filming* 329 (February 1982): 23-24.
Finds the film a telling picture of American injustice because it presents the contrasting fates of Harry Thaw and Coalhouse Walker. The film further suggests that the spirit of the times affects people; they are not independently heroes or villians.

446 Gelmis, Joseph. Review in *Newsday*, 20 November 1981, Part II, 3.
Praises the film as one of the best in 1981 because it effectively recreates the era's diverse elements and its characters' lives are authentic. Calls casting "ingenious."

447 Gertner, Richard. "*Ragtime*: A Feast for the Eyes With Performances Worthy of an Oscar." *Motion Picture Product Digest* 9 (11 November 1981), 45-46.
Believes the film works aesthetically and dramatically, and its success may dispel the myth that period films cannot work. Praises Forman's decisions on plot, characterizations, and acting.

448 Gussow, Mel. "Altman Goes by the Book--His Way." *The New York Times*, 24 February 1976, 28.
An account of Altman's plans for filming *Ragtime* and Vonnegut's *Breakfast of Champions*.

449 Harmetz, Aljean. "When Emma Goldman Hit the Cutting-Room Floor." *The New York Times*, 12 December 1981, 21.
Reports on Forman's decision to omit scenes including Goldman from the film.

450   Hatch, Robert.   Review in *Nation* 233 (12 December
       1981), 650-651.
            Says the filmscript "operates" on the book and
       focuses on its central cord--the Coalhouse Walker
       subplot.   Thus the film is more serious than the novel
       and has a narrower scope.   Finds irony in a black
       actor's losing top billing to James Cagney.

451   Higham, Charles.   "How *Ragtime* Led to Discord."   *The
       New York Times*, 26 September 1976, Section 2, 1+.
            Tells of disagreements between Altman, Doctorow
       and others who are involved in making the film.
       Reports that problems started when Altman assigned
       the directorship to Miloš Foreman.

452   Jacobs, Diane.   "Making Books."   *Horizon* 24 (December
       1981), 70-71.
            Believes the first forty minutes of the film cap-
       ture the novel's panoramic style, but the rest of the
       movie focuses on Coalhouse Walker, who is the em-
       bodiment of liberal guilt rather than a flesh and blood
       person.   Hence, the film progressively weakens.

453   Jefferson, Margo.   *Ms.* 10 (February 1982), 25, 28.
            Says the film lacks the novel's psychological
       and historical context, omits interesting characters,
       and trivializes the characters it includes.

454   Johnson, Herschel.   "Howard Rollins Jr. Hits the Big
       Time in *Ragtime*."   *Essence* 12 (January 1982), 13.
            Brief biography of actor who played Coalhouse
       Walker.   He is quoted as saying Coalhouse and his
       comrades believe in something, and such conviction is
       rarely portrayed in films.

455   Kael, Pauline.   The Current Cinema.   *The New Yorker*,
       57 (23 November 1981), 176-185.
            Reviews *Ragtime* with several other films.
       Believes that the novel had a wide appeal to
       Americans who had a historical sense of the ragtime
       era.   The Czech director Miloš Forman, however,
       lacked this sense of American history and sensibility;
       consequently, *Ragtime* is a dull movie.

456   Kauffmann, Stanley.   "Turning the Century."   *New
       Republic* 185 (2 December 1981), 24-26.
            Argues that while the novel successfully
       adapted the film methods of Renoir and Kurosawa, the

film itself is a stylized, conventional Hollywood movie
that cannot replicate the book's sense of history.

'457   Kennedy, Harlan.   "*Ragtime*: Milos Forman Searching
for the Right Key."   *American Film: The Magazine of
the Film and Television Arts* 7 (December 1981): 38-43.
        Discusses the film's challenge to Forman.
Focusses on Forman's view that the film cannot be a
literal adaptation of the novel and that his biggest
challenges were making the characters concrete and
capturing the elliptical nature of the novel.   Includes
information on Howard Rollins, who played Coalhouse
Walker.

458   Kroll, Jack.   "Ragtime in Waltz Time."   *Newsweek* 98
(23 November 1981), 124.
        Says the film is marred by a lack of vision,
energy and passion.   Feels that in an attempt to
achieve a mythic quality, the acting is often dulled.

459   Linnett, Richard.   Review in *Cineaste* 12 (1982): 52-53.
        Believes that the film is entertaining, but it is
dominated by the Coalhouse Walker subplot.   Since
Coalhouse Walker's plight does not represent that of
most black Americans, his story plays to emotions
rather than facts.

460   McMurtry, Larry.   "On Ragged Time Knit Up Thy
Ragged Sleeve."   *American Film: The Magazine of the
Film and Television Arts* 2 (December 1976/January
1977): 4-5.
        Contends it is impossible for a Hollywood movie
to be a work of art.   Believes Doctorow should be
more sophisticated and realize this, but the author
shouldn't worry about the film adaptation because the
novel is a separate entity that can't be dampened by
a movie version.

461   Nachman, Gerald.   "*Ragtime*: Real Portrait of America."
San Francisco Chronicle, 20 November 1981, 65.
        Says this film captures the essence of the
American dream of upward mobility and as well as its
price.   It further depicts the plights of blacks.
Reviewer compares both the film and the book to Dos
Passos's work, in that all juxtapose the lives of the
famous with those of unknowns.

462 Pulleine, Tim. "Fact and Fiction." *Sight and Sound: The International Film Quarterly* 51 (Winter 1981/1982): 134.
     Argues that the novel depended on a complex sort of literary allusion that cannot be translated into film. Thus the film requires viewers to trust its seemingly inexplicable character motivation and narrative logic.

463 Quart, Leonard and Barbara. "*Ragtime* Without a Melody." *Literature/Film Quarterly* 10 (1982): 71–74.
     Maintains that although the film attempts fidelity to the novel, it fails to capture the book's political consciousness and metaphoric complexity.

464 Reed, Rex. Review in *Daily News*, 23 November 1981, 38.
     Believes the film fails because it lacks a coherent plot and momentum. Calls the novel a film in itself.

465 Review in *Cinema*. 277 (January 1982): 64–66.
     Concludes the film is long, artificial and filled with images lacking apparent purpose; overall, *Ragtime* is a sorry representation of Forman's talent. (in French)

466 Review in *Variety*, 18 November 1981, 14.
     Says Forman captures the essence of the novel and stays close to its entertaining, kaleidoscopic style. Praises the script, acting, musical score and production.

467 Sarris, Andrew. Review in *Village Voice*, 18–24 November 1981, 57.
     States that the film is far preferable to the novel, which had strained literary allusions and did not accurately capture the period. Has mixed feelings about the film's casting.

468 Schlesinger, Arthur Jr. "History and the Imagination: *Ragtime* and *Reds*." *American Heritage: The Magazine of History*. 33 (April/May 1982): 42–43.
     Compares and contrasts these two historical films, stating that while *Ragtime* evades history by leaving out the book's panoramic vision, *Reds* revels in it, particularly by interviewing people from the period.

469 Serceau, Michel. "A Travers l'Historie a Galop." La
Revue du Cinema 373 (June 1982): 24-29.
Reviews with *Reds* and *Georgia*. Compares the
three films on such matters as their treatment of
major characters and their portrayals of American justice. Suggests Younger Brother prefigures the
American radical of the 1960s.

470 Sharp, Christopher. *Women's Wear Daily*, 17 November
1981, 16.
States that by concentrating on the Coalhouse
Walker subplot, the film suggests future violence,
while the novel suggested past events. Believes the
film is not as good as book, but the movie does
succeed on its own terms.

471 Simon, John. "Wrong-Note Rag." *National Review: A
Journal of Fact and Opinion* 34 (5 February 1982),
122-123.
Says the movie fails because it lacks the novel's
kaleidoscopic vision. The dominance of the Coalhouse
Walker subplot only reveals this episode's inferiority
to the Kleist story that inspired it. Performances are
uneven.

472 Smith, Ronn. "Organizing *Ragtime*: Art Direction of
the Film." *Theatre Crafts* 16 (January 1982): 17, 43-
47.
Tells of how necessary strict organization and
planning is in making a film such as *Ragtime*, which is
set in fifty-four locations on two continents.

473 Sobchack, Tom. "*Ragtime*: An Improvisation on Hollywood Style." *Literature/Film Quarterly* 13 (1985):
148-154.
States that while the movie *Ragtime* had a wide
popular appeal, it actually went against the grain of
Hollywood movies, much as ragtime music violated the
conventions of traditional popular music. The movie
was unconventional because its narrative was choppy
and its characters were unpredictable.

474 Sragow, Michael. Review in *Rolling Stone*, 18 February
1982, 28.
Calls this film one of the worst literary adaptations ever. Characters are flattened, Forman's depiction of upper-class life suggests a doctrinaire view of
the class struggle, and the social implications of
Coalhouse's struggle are missing.

475 Sterritt, David. "Miloš Forman and the Tricky Business of Filming *Ragtime*." *The Christian Science
Monitor*, 10 December 1981, 19.
      Praises the screenplay, but finds the film less
radical than the book. Explains Forman's rationale for
cutting parts. Discusses Forman's view that
Coalhouse's problem is his hurt pride, and explores
the challenge of making a serious film in a commercial
environment.

476 Thomson, David. "Redtime." *Film Comment* 18
(January/February 1982): 11-16.
      Reviews with *Reds*. Praises Foreman for his su-
perb selection of events from the novel. Is especially
impressed by the film's suggestion of the relationship
between love and money and its depiction of Mother's
awakening.

477 Westerbeck, Colin L. Jr. "Rags to Revolution: History
and the Romantic Vision." *Commonweal* 109 (12
February 1982), 87-89.
      Says *Ragtime* compares favorably to *Reds* be-
cause the former is entertaining and faithful to the
novel. Believes Doctorow's novel itself is a parody of
a Hugoesque book about human relationships.

478 Wolf, William. "When a Book Becomes a Movie." *New
York*, 30 November 1981, 66-67.
      Explores why so many film adaptations, such as
Ragtime, are unsuccessful. Suggests conflicts between
creators and producers, conflicts between producers
and directors and commercial considerations.

Film

479 *Daniel*. Directed by Sidney Lumet. Produced by
Burtt Harris. Screenplay by E.L. Doctorow, Paramount
Pictures, 1983.

Reviews

480 Anderson, Pat. Review in *Films in Review* 34
(October 1983): 500-501.
      Sees this film as the saga of a young man
trying to come to terms with his special place in history. Finds Lumet's direction brilliantly original,
Robeson's songs particularly effective and the casting
perfect.

481 Ansen, David. "The Children of the Damned."
 Newsweek 102 (29 August 1983), 65.
 Says the movie fails because it lacks focus.
 Daniel's journey is not introduced until halfway into
 the film, and episodes from the past and present are
 included without apparent purpose.

482 Arnold, Gary. "Uneven *Daniel:* Fact Fights Fiction in
 Doctorow Adaptation." *The Washington Post*, 23 September 1983, E1, 8.
 Finds film strongest in depicting scenes from
 Jewish lower-middle class and Communist life in 1930s
 through 1950s, weakest (almost melodramatic) in its
 depiction of the couple's fate. The discontinuous narrative is hard to follow, and the acting is uneven.

483 Asahina, Robert. "Reviving the Rosenberg Affair."
 New Leader 66 (3 October 1983), 20–21.
 Finds the movie lacks the book's implications of
 the couple's guilt and its criticisms of both the Old
 and New Left. Suggests in the Reagan era liberals
 have become fearful and sentimental about their pasts.

484 Benson, Sheila. Review in *Los Angeles Times*, 23 September 1983, Calendar 1.
 Says that although there are some moments of
 fine acting, the film ultimately fails. Neither Doctorow
 nor Lumet addresses the issue of the couple's guilt,
 and the film is sentimental.

485 Bosworth, Patricia. "Movie With a Conscience." *Work-
 ing Woman* 8 (September 1983), 232–234.
 Explores Lumet's interest in making this film.
 Evaluates the film's acting as fine, the film on the
 whole as superb.

486 Buckley, Peter. "Labor of Love." *Horizon* 26
 (September 1983), 45–49.
 Reports on the intense commitment of the director and actors and actresses involved in making this
 film.

487 Chase, Donald. "Reassembling the Face of New York."
 Theatre Crafts 17 (November/December 1983): 28–30,
 38–41.
 Tells how the production designer staged the
 set design in New York for *Daniel*'s three different
 time periods.

488   Coleman, John. Review in *New Statesman* 107 (13
       January 1984), 30.
             Commends the film of novel he believed impos-
       sible to film. Says the movie captures the book's
       political climate and personal torment with amazing ac-
       curacy.

489   Colpart, Gilles. "*Daniel*: Le Procès d´une Société
       Malade." *La Revue du Cinema* 392 (March 1984): 34-35.
             Praises the film's tough intelligence, mastery of
       material and implicit comparison of the past and
       present.

490   Combs, Richard. "Out of the Lion's Den." *Sight and
       Sound: The International Film Quarterly* 53 (Winter
       1983/84): 63-64.
             Says the film lacks narrative energy, a sense of
       drama and development. Criticizes Lumet's decision to
       shoot all Isaacson scenes in filtered orange and all
       late-1960s scenes in color.

491   Corliss, Richard. "Romance of the Rosenbergs." *Time*
       122 (29 August 1983), 61.
             Suggests the film excuses Communists and fails
       because good actors and actresses are given stifling
       roles. Finds rhetoric of the film both fierce and sen-
       timental.

492   Denby, David. "A Communist Romance." *New York* 35
       (5 September 1983), 49-50.
             Accuses Doctorow and Lumet of altering the
       facts of the Rosenberg case only when doing so sug-
       gests the couple's innocence. Says the novel's anger
       and complexity are flattened in the film; flashbacks
       to 1930s are sentimentalized.

493   Farber, Stephen. Review in *Film Quarterly* 37 (Spring
       1984): 32-37.
             Says the film is better than the critics indicate
       and attributes the poor reviews to a resurgence of
       anti-Communist feeling. Compares *Daniel* to films such
       as *The Grapes of Wrath* in which a family's destruc-
       tion epitomizes its era's wrongs.

494   Gelmis, Joseph. Review in *Newsday*, 26 August 1983,
       Part 2, 3.
             Believes the movie is weak because its charac-
       ters, like the novel's, are not admirable and thus the
       viewers cannot care about them. Also comments on

the film's focus on family life at the expense of historical context.

495 Goodman, Jean. "The Rosenberg Case." *Observer*, 8 January 1984, 54.
     Gives background information on the Rosenberg case and discusses the continuing controversy over it which is partially reflected in the controversy over the film. Discusses how Radosh's book (see item 527) has fueled debate.

496 Grenier, Richard. "The Hard Left and the Soft." *Commentary* 77 (January 1984), 56-61.
     Reviews *Daniel* and four other political films. Believes the publication of *The Rosenberg File*, asserting Julius Rosenberg's guilt, soon before *Daniel's* release damaged the film's reception, but the film probably would have failed anyway because it is unabashedly sentimental about Stalinist Communists.

497 Howe, Irving. "The Troubles of *Daniel*." *Dissent* 31 (Winter 1984): 121-123.
     Argues that the film is marred by a particular kind of political sensibility which sentimentalizes the Old Left American Communists. Those with this sensibility intellectually realize that the Communist movement was evil, although many of the Jewish immigrants who were drawn to it were good; but emotionally the sympathizers cannot reconcile these two realities. Political judgments are thus muddled, and *Daniel* is marred by a similar inability to take a stand on the accused couple's guilt or innocence.

498 Insdorf, Annette. "Lumet Behind the Lens." *Harper's Bazaar* 116 (September 1983), 347+.
     Focusses on Lumet's political ideology and his interest in making this film.

499 Jaehne, Karen. Review in *Cineaste* 13 (1984): 35-37.
     Sees the film as an effective rendition of the crimes of the Cold War era and people's helplessness when caught in political machinations. Says Lumet generally stages good shots and avoids easy outs, but the ending is implausible and it lacks the complexity of the novel's endings.

500 Kael, Pauline. Review in *The New Yorker* 59 (5 September 1983), 109-111.
     Criticizes the film as an upsetting fantasy that

tries to exploit the fears of Jews and leftists. Because Daniel never directly asks if his parents were
guilty, his search seems pointless.
Rebuttal in item 511.

501 Kart, Larry. "A Left-Wing Soap Opera? Controversial
Daniel Aims for More." *Chicago Tribune*, 25 September
1983, Section 12, 5-6.
Discusses Lumet's and Doctorow's goals in
making the film and the critics' negative, often angry,
responses to *Daniel*.

502 Kauffmann, Stanley. "Wrestling Society for a Soul."
New Republic 189 (12 September 1983), 24.
Finds screenplay severely reductive. Unlike the
novel, the film is not ostensibly Daniel's book and it
lacks Biblical allusions. Thus the film does not
resonate. Reviewer believes Doctorow extracts scenes
from his novel with little sense of purpose.

503 Kempley, Rita. "*Daniel:* Heavy Going in the Gloom."
Washington Post, 23 September 1983, Weekend, 21.
Concludes film has some strong, moving scenes,
but they are too disjointed to affect viewers. Scenes
of Daniel talking about execution and torture should
have been cut.

504 Kihss, Peter. "The Movie *Daniel:* How Close Is It to
History?" *The New York Times*, 31 August 1983, C21.
Summarizes the similarities and differences be-
tween the film and the actual Rosenberg case.

505 Kissel, Howard. Review in *Women's Wear Daily*, 17
August 1983, 34.
Praises the film for its effective juxtaposition of
past and present, its good direction and many
memorable, moving scenes.

506 Maslin, Janet. "*Daniel*, a Question of Justice." *The
New York Times*, 26 August 1983, C10.
Finds the film more ponderous and less pas-
sionate than the novel, partially because the film
focuses on the couple while the novel deals with the
more interesting question of what becomes of their
offspring. Says actors are poorly cast.
Rebuttal in item 511.

507 ------. "*Daniel* Confuses More Than One Issue." *The
New York Times*, 4 September 1983, Section 2, 11-12.

States the film's mingling of fact and fiction is unsuccessful. Furthermore finds the characters' tendency to give speeches makes the film seem polemical and misses a sense of the texture of the Isaacsons' lives.
Rebuttal in item 511.

508 Mason, Deborah. "'Daniel': Love and Protest." *Vogue* 173 (August 1983), 318-321, 378.
Describes the familial atmosphere in filming the movie and the actors' and actresses' commitment.

509 Milne, Tom. Review in *Monthly Film Bulletin* 51 (January 1984): 8-9.
Finds acting and direction superb, but sees the last scene as a manipulative, hollow gesture of protest affirmation.

510 O'Toole, Lawrence. "The Two Greatest Losses in the World." *Macleans* 96 (3 October 1983), 61.
Finds the film powerful and moving. Praises its unsentimental depiction of the two great losses--those of home and identity--which the Isaacson children suffer. Faults Daniel's character for being "whitewashed," however, and finds the film's ending weak.

511 Pollitt, Katha. Review in *Nation* 237 (1 October 1983), 283-285.
Finds many reviewers' criticisms of sudden flashes in time and implausible ending valid, but suspects film would have been greeted differently in a less stridently anti-Communist age and before the publication of Ronald Radosh's *The Rosenberg File*.
Refers to items 500, 506, 507, 513.

512 Review in *Variety*, 24 August 1983, 14.
Finds movie curiously detached, marred by poor casting and visually ugly.

513 Sarris, Andrew. "The Rosenbergs, the Isaacsons and Thou." *Village Voice*, 6 September 1983, 45, 51.
Calls the film visually ugly and believes it fails on every level. The book's wit and ambiguity are missing; Doctorow and Lumet glorify Communists and ignore the Reds' wrongdoings.
Rebuttal in item 511.

514 Schneir, Miriam. "Lindsay Crouse and *Daniel*." Ms. 12
(November 1983), 38–42.
    Discusses aspects of movie rather than critiques
them. Focuses on Lindsay Crouse's powerful performance as Rochelle Isaacson and outlines Crouse's
politics. Also pinpoints resemblances between the film
and the actual Rosenberg case.

515 Seitz, Michael H. "Deaths in the Family." *Progressive*
47 (November 1983): 36.
    Finds the mingling of fact and fiction confusing,
the casting sometimes inappropriate and the crowd
scenes contrived. Admires the film's politics and ambition, but believes it fails.

516 Simon, John. "Simple, But Not Good." *National
Review: A Journal of Fact and Opinion* 35 (14 October
1983), 1294, 1296.
    Believes the film fails on almost all levels. Its
plot distorts the facts of the Rosenberg case, its
scenes lack subtlety and its casting is inappropriate.

517 Sinyard, Neil. Review in *Films & Filming* 354 (March
1984): 40–41.
    Finds film visually predictable and lacking in
character development.

518 Sterritt, David. "Amid the Trivia of a Poor Season, a
Complex and Challenging Drama." *The Christian
Science Monitor*, 1 September 1983, 16.
    Praises this film as a serious drama and says
its casting is good. Feels, however, that techniques
such as shifts in time, that worked well in the novel,
fail in the film. Ultimately, the book is better.

519 ------. "E.L. Doctorow's Collaboration with the
Enemy." *The Christian Science Monitor*, 13 October
1983, 29–30.
    Discusses Doctorow's collaboration on the film
and his writing the screenplay in view of his belief
that film has contributed to illiteracy. Reports on
Doctorow's statement that he has used the idea of the
Rosenberg case rather than written about the actual
couple. Also mentions Doctorow's conviction that
Americans should examine their national myths.

520 Stone, Judy. "Ambitious Film Falls Short." *San Francisco Chronicle*, 23 September 1983, 70.
    Praises the film's ambition, but believes

Doctorow's goal of trying to depict the Left's complex sacrificial role in America could not be accomplished on film.

III

SELECTED SUPPLEMENTARY BIBLIOGRAPHY

THE ROSENBERG CASE: BACKGROUND MATERIAL

Books

521 Gardner, Virginia. *The Rosenberg Story*. New York:
Masses and Mainstream, 1954.
  Tells the story of Ethel's and Julius's lives
before their arrests. Extols the couple and adds to
the image of them as martyrs.

522 Meeropol, Robert and Michael. *We Are Your Sons: The
Legacy of Ethel and Julius Rosenberg*. Boston:
Houghton Mifflin Co., 1975.
  An autobiography of the Rosenbergs' children in
which they tell of their parents' arrests and execu-
tions, their subsequent lives and their decision to
reveal their Rosenberg identities. This book strongly
asserts the Rosenbergs' innocence.
Written partially in reaction to item 524.

523 National Committee to Secure Justice in the Rosenberg
Case. *New Evidence in the Rosenberg Case*. New
York: National Committee..., 1953.
  Pamphlet claiming that some newly-found
government memos indicate that the Rosenbergs are
innocent.

524 Nizer, Louis. *The Implosion Conspiracy*. New York:
Doubleday & Co, 1973.
  Written by a lawyer who believes the Rosenbergs were guilty. The story of the trial is
presented in a manner meant to persuade the reader.
Nizer begins his account by claiming the Rosenberg
story was not only the extraordinary spy story of
century; it was also an extraordinary love story.
Nizer also focuses on the Rosenbergs' family life and
the couple's personalities.

525 Pilat, Oliver. *The Atom Spies.* New York: G.P. Putnam and Sons, 1952.

      Narrative assumes guilt of Rosenbergs and other atom spies were guilty and presents its material in the form of a popular spy novel. Throughout the book, it is implied that Communism is a pernicious influence.

526 Radosh, Ronald and Joyce Milton. *The Rosenberg File: A Search for the Truth.* New York: Holt, Rinehart and Winston, 1983.

      Re-examination of Rosenberg case using FBI files previously closed but now available under the Freedom of Information Act. Radosh purportedly began this research under the assumption that the Rosenbergs were innocent, but by examining these newly available documents, he became convinced that Julius was guilty and Ethel was a likely accomplice. This book refueled the controversy around the case. Discussed in items 150, 495, 528.

527 Rosenberg, Ethel and Julius. *Death House Letters of Ethel and Julius Rosenberg.* New York: Jero Publishing Company, 1953.

      Letters written by the Rosenbergs during their imprisonment. This correspondence indicates their love for one another and for their children It also offers insight into their attitude toward the legal process and their impending executions. Referred to in item 550.

528 Schneir, Walter and Miriam. *Invitation to an Inquest.* 2nd. ed. New York: Pantheon Books, 1983.

      The definitive book arguing for the Rosenbergs' innocence. Begins with background information on how the atom bomb was developed and argues that America had a desire to keep a nuclear monopoly. Further claims that there were no atomic secrets, and the Rosenbergs were victims of a hysterical political climate.
This edition also refutes some points made in item 526.

529 Sharp, Malcolm. *Was Justice Done? The Rosenberg-Sobell Case.* New York: Monthly Review Press, 1956.

      Contends that the Rosenberg were innocent. Argues his case by disputing the court record and questioning the validity of accomplice testimony in general.

530 Wexley, John. *The Judgment of Julius and Ethel
     Rosenberg.* 2nd. ed. New York: Ballantyne Books, 1977.
       Argues for the Rosenbergs' innocence and em-
     phasizes seeming injustices in the trial.

Articles and Letters

531 Adams, Caroline. "The Rosenberg Case." *Commonweal*
     58 (4 September 1953), 538–539.
       States Americans believed in the Rosenbergs'
     guilt and the couple received due process of law.
     Rebuttal to item 533.

532 "An American Failure." *Nation* 176 (27 June 1953),
     533–535.
       Sees the Rosenbergs' execution as a failure of
     American justice and the nation's conscience.

533 Barrat, Robert. "From France: The Rosenberg Case."
     Commonweal 58 (14 August 1953), 464–466.
       Attributes France's sympathy for the
     Rosenbergs to comparisons with the Dreyfus affair and
     the French people's view that the couple were
     scapegoats for anti-Communist hysteria.
     Rebutted in item 531.

534 "The Crime and Punishment of Julius and Ethel
     Rosenberg." *New Republic* 128 (29 June 1953), 6.
       Says the Rosenbergs were probably guilty and
     the Communist Party probably benefited from their
     apparent martyrdom. Regrets that the Supreme Court
     never fully confirmed the legality of the death
     penalty.

535 Editorial in *Nation* 176 (28 February 1953), 179.
       Criticizes Eisenhower's decision to deny
     clemency.

536 Fiedler, Leslie. "Afterthoughts on the Rosenbergs."
     In *An End to Innocence: Essays on Culture and
     Politics.* 1955. Reprint. New York: Stein and Day,
     1972, 25–45.
       Believes the Rosenbergs were guilty, but is
     more interested in the nature of the Rosenberg case.
     Says there were two Rosenberg cases; the actual case,
     which was uninteresting; and the symbolic case, which
     captured the world's interest because it presented the
     couple as martyrs.

537 Fineberg, S. Andhl. "Plain Facts About the Rosenberg Case." *Reader's Digest* 63 (September 1953), 9-14.
     Defends the death sentence and praises Judge Kauffman for imposing it. Says many eminent people without legal training were seduced by Communist propaganda.

538 "France and the Rosenbergs." *Nation* 177 (4 July 1953), 1.
     Editorial attributes the pro-Rosenberg sentiment in France to a fear that America is acting out of repressive anti-Communist hysteria.

539 Hays, Arthur Garfield. "The Rosenberg Case." *Nation* 175 (8 November 1952), 422-423.
     Believes the Rosenbergs were guilty, but finds the death sentence unwarranted.

540 Hoover, J. Edgar. "The Crime of the Century." *Reader's Digest* 58 (May 1951), 149-168.
     Gives an account of Klaus Fuchs and Harry Gold's interactions that is highly dramatic and suggests Communism's power to blind people's moral judgment.

541 "It Could Never Happen in Russia: How Law Protected the Rights of the Rosenbergs." *U.S. News & World Report* 34 (26 June 1953), 32-35.
     Stresses the fairness of America's judicial process.

542 Kirchwey, Freda. "Mercy for the Rosenbergs." *Nation* 176 (10 January 1953), 24.
     Argues that the Rosenbergs should not be executed even if they gave atomic secrets to the Soviet Union because the Soviets were a United States ally during the latter part of World War II.

543 *Newsweek* 41 (23 February 1953), 50.
     Gives a very condensed account of Eisenhower's refusal to grant clemency, the Pope's plea for mercy and the Court of Appeals decision to defer the execution.

544 "Payment Deferred." *Newsweek* 41 (26 January 1953), 42.
     Says Communist propaganda, which was absent during the Rosenberg trial, became apparent when the death sentence was pronounced. Also states that a

tactic often used by propagandists was to charge that anti-Semitism had tainted the case.

545   "Regarding the Rosenbergs." *Commonweal* 57 (9 January 1953), 344.
      States that the Rosenbergs are bringing about their own deaths by their stubborn refusal to to confess and cooperate with authorities.

546   "The Rosenberg Case." *Commonweal* 59 (26 February 1954), 529–530.
      Does not dispute the conviction or the death sentence, but fears Americans' desire for vengeance on Communists. Pleads with Americans to fight Communism by fighting the economic and social conditions that attract people to it.

547   *Time* 60 (1 December 1952), 22.
      Claims that Communists are behind the charges of anti-Semitism in the case.

548   *Time* 61 (12 January 1953), 21.
      Summarizes the case.

549   *Time* 61 (29 June 1953), 7–10.
      States that Americans did not execute the Rosenbergs in anti-Communist hysteria, but had sound reasons to be convinced of their guilt. The death sentence for treason was warranted.

550   Warshow, Robert. "The 'Idealism' of Julius and Ethel Rosenberg: The Kind of People We Are." *Commentary* 16 (November 1953), 413–418.
      Analyzes some of the death house letters (item 527) to determine how the Rosenbergs could betray their country, yet apparently face death with a clear conscience. Sees the couple's actions as exemplifying the Communism of the early 1950s.

551   "The Week: The Rosenberg Case." *New Republic* 128 (19 January 1953), 7.
      Agrees that the Rosenbergs are guilty, but finds the death sentence too harsh and urges it be commuted for the sake of world opinion.

552   "Who Sentenced the Rosenbergs?" *Nation* 176 (20 June 1953), 513.
      Editorial argues that the Rosenbergs were

convicted by McCarthyite anti-Communist hysteria, not the judicial process.

553 "Wrong--'By a Damn Sight.'" *Newsweek* 43 (1 March 1954), 72.
　　　Disagrees with the analysis of the Rosenberg case conducted by Columbia University law students who concluded that in its last stages Case did not get due consideration from the Supreme Court.

Dissertation

554 Powell, Jerry Owen. "The Structure of Narrative: Facts and Fiction of the Rosenberg Case." Dissertation, Indiana University, 1981.
　　　Examines versions of the Rosenberg case in news magazines, books, newspapers and fiction, with an eye to how form influences content.
　　　See item 163.

Newspaper Coverage

555 *The New York Times.* Coverage of the Rosenberg Case from 24 May 1950 through 30 December 1953.

Literary Adaptations

556 Coover, Robert. *The Public Burning.* New York: Viking Press, 1967.
　　　Inspired by the Rosenberg case, this novel focusses on the character of Richard Nixon.

557 Freed, Donald. *Inquest: A Play.* New York: Hill and Wang, 1969.
　　　Drama closely adapts the Rosenberg case. The introduction says the Rosenbergs were victims of an American myth of virtue and patriotism, and the play presents an anti-myth exposing the myth's perniciousness.

IV

ADDITIONAL SOURCES

Additional Sources

Book Reviews

558 Review of *World's Fair.* In *Books & Bookmen* 364 (February 1986): 18+.

Film Reviews

Ragtime

559 *American Cinematographer* 63 (May 1982): 450+.

560 Amiel, V. *Positif* 278 (April 1984): 75.

561 Bouheraoua, F. "*Ragtime*" *Deux Ecrans* 49 (October 1982): 3-4.

562 Branford, M. "The Story Behind *Ragtime.*" *Photoplay* 33 (March 1982): 18-21.

563 Celemenski, M. *Cinematographe* 74 (January 1982): 34-36.

564 Dickstein, M. "Time Bandits." *American Film* 8 (October 1982): 39-43.

565 *Film* 115 (April/May 1983): 18.

566 *Film Kritik* 26 (February 1982): 95-96.

567 Garel, A. *Revue du Cinema* 26 (1982): 284-285.

568 Gervais, G. *Jeune Cinema* 140 (February 1982): 31-34.

569 Kloeck, E. *Andere Sinema* 38 (April 1982): 37-38.

570 Kornis, M. "Zongorista a Hazteton." *Film Vilag* 28 (1985): 10-11.

571 Link, J. "The Screening Room." *American Premiere* 2 (December/January 1981/1982): 60-61.

572 Nacarache, J. *Cinema 82* 277 (January 1982): 64-66.

573 Rothenbuechen, B. *Christian Century* 98 (16 December 1981), 1322.

574 Shupp, P. *Sequences* 108 (April 1982): 26-27.

575 Smith, D. *Photoplay Movies and Video,* 26 March 1982, 33.

Additional Sources

576 Summers, J. *Boxoffice* 118 (January 1982): 51–53.

577 Wells, J. *Film Journal* 85 (10 December 1981), 10.

Daniel

578 Chevrie, M. *Cahiers du Cinema* 357 (March 1984): 55–56.

579 Combs, R. "Delivering *Daniel.*" *Monthly Film Bulletin* 51 (January 1984): 10–11.

580 Connolly, K. *Cinema Papers* 47 (August 1984): 270–271.

581 Dewson, L. "How *Daniel* Was Thrown to the Lion of Politics." *Photoplay* 35 (February 1984): 43–45.

582 Dhont, F. and J. MacTrevor. *Cinema Revue* 64 (1 March 1984): 10–13.

583 Gervais, G. *Jeune Cinema* 158 (April 1984): 47–48.

584 Girard, M. *Sequences* 115 (January 1984): 61–62.

585 Gray, M. *Photoplay* 35 (February 1984): 20.

586 Kock, I. de. *Andere Sinema* 59 (May/June 1984): 36.

587 Martin, M. *Revue du Cinema* 24 (1984): 45–46.

588 McVay, D. *Film* 121 (December 1983): 1+.

589 Salomonsen, S. "Historiens Gentagelse: 'Var de Skylidge.'" *Kosmorama* 30 (1984): 158–161.

590 Summers, J. *Boxoffice* 119 (November 1983), 49.

Articles

591 Estrin, Barbara. "Recomposing Time: *Humboldt's Gift* and *Ragtime.*" *Denver Quarterly* 17 (Spring 1982): 16–31.

NAME INDEX

Name Index

TITLE INDEX